LEARNING TO COUNT WHAT REALLY COUNTS

THE ECONOMICS OF WHOLENESS

TOM BENDER

FIRE RIVER PRESS

PUBLISHED BY ──────

FIRE RIVER PRESS
PO Box 397
Manzanita OR 97130 USA
email: fireriverpress@nehalemtel.net

FIRE RIVER PRESS books by the same author:

ENVIRONMENTAL DESIGN PRIMER, 1973
THE HEART OF PLACE, 1993
SILENCE, SONG, AND SHADOWS, 2000
BUILDING WITH THE BREATH OF LIFE, 2000
LEARNING TO COUNT
    WHAT *REALLY* COUNTS, 2002

LIBRARY OF CONGRESS CONTROL NUMBER: 2001119461
Bender, Tom
    LEARNING TO COUNT WHAT *REALLY* COUNTS:
    The Economics of Wholeness/
    by Tom Bender
    Includes index and bibliographical references
ISBN 0-9675089-2-4
    1. Economics - forecasting - principles
    2. Systems - connected
    3. Values
    4. Ecology
    5. Factor 10
    6. Chi Energy
    7. Sustainability

*P*REFACE

It gives me shivers even now, reading proofs of the last pages of this book – about religious fundamentalism and terrorism. The manuscript was finished on September 6, 2001, five days *before* the World Trade Center and the Pentagon were bombed.

I had awakened one morning this summer with an urgent sense that I needed to write this book, and to have it finished by the first of September. I was puzzled – there were already two excellent books about Factor Ten Economics, which I had pioneered more than 25 years ago. But the outline for the book was etched on the back of my mind, and the urgency wouldn't go away.

As I began writing, part of the answer became clear. The existing books focused primarily on the resource productivity aspect of Factor Ten. How to have more stuff, with less environmental impact. That was safe, and important, and probably the best route to the amazing acceptance that Factor Ten is receiving. But there seemed a compelling need now to focus on its deeper aspects. The role and vast benefits from values and the sacred (dare we speak of such things in a book about economics?) *Multiple* order-of-magnitude improvements possible in institutional and financial performance, in personal and social well-being, and in planetary health and goals. How totally different it feels to live within this new economics. Whether these amazing improvements might be a one-shot deal. What we should do with this wonderful gift.

After September 11, the answer seems clear. Factor Ten economics gives us means to make the whole world a success – to end poverty, starvation, and battles over resources. We've seen enough of the results of greed. It's time now for compassion and sharing. Putting economics in service to creating the best world we can imagine – for all. I humbly pass on these words to you, with a prayer that they may help us see, and move towards, what is possible.

Tom Bender - 30 Oct. 2001

For Bucky and Fritz

Illustration Credits:

p11,112, 115 - by Diane Schatz, from BUILDING VALUE, California Office of State Architect; p16,23, 43, 46, 55, 59, 72, 73, 75, 99, 127, 133, 163, 164, 175 by the author; p25 - Revolution, courtesy of Hypercar, Inc.; p29, 53, 54 - by Diane Schatz, Office of Energy Research and Planning, State of Oregon; p98 - Frog Hollow Farm Worker Housing, courtesy Dan Smith and Associates, Architects - www.dsaarch.com; p124 - Gaviotas Hospital Solar Kitchen, excerpted from GAVIOTAS, by Alan Weisman, ©1998, with permission from Chelsea Green Publishing, White River Junction VT - www.chelseagreen.com, 1-800-639-4099; p129 - after DEFLATION, by A. Gary Schilling; p144 from THE DRAWINGS OF HEINRICH KLEY, Dover Publications, 1960; p160 -RAIN Urban Renewal Poster, by Diane Schatz.

COVER Image: GAIA - by Alice Kelley, www.AliceKelley.com

Contents

Chapter 1
The Economics of Wholeness

This book is about a revolution occurring today in economics. It is not a big book, because it doesn't take a lot to show the benefits of what is occurring. It is not filled with mathematics and complex equations, because the changes that are transforming economics today are not involved with the sophisticated calculation and modeling which has been so central to recent economics.

The dramatic changes affecting economics today lie in three areas:

* *Meta-economics*, the relationship between economics and the *larger* social and ecological systems of which it is part. Immense improvement in effectiveness of our social and industrial systems is being achieved today through new insights into the connection of these systems, and more direct ways to attain our deepest goals. This is in contrast to *micro*-economics which has been the prime focus of economics in recent years, focusing on computerized modeling and fine-tuning of traditional economic perspectives.

* *Bridge-economics*, the interface between economics and other parts of our world – simple yet penetrating concepts that bridge between disciplines, and which bring powerful new insights developed in other disciplines to bear on issues of economics.

* *Whole-system economics*, defining the boundaries of analysis to include the whole interactive web of costs and benefits of

alternative actions, and developing measurement tools that properly account true costs and benefits.

Together, developments in these areas are bringing *order-of-magnitude* improvement in the way we operate our businesses and institutions and handle our lives. They are achieving ten-fold improvements *no only* in resource productivity, but also in institutional and financial productivity, personal and social goals and well-being, and in social and planetary welfare. Most excitingly, they offer unprecedented hope for the well-being and happiness of *all* of us living on this planet.

The transformations emerging through this new "economics of wholeness" are portentously appropriate to the issues facing our world today. Big changes are in the works, and they are a way to help make those changes positive ones.

The principles of the new economics are uncomplicated, and understandable in plain English. Which is appropriate, because one of the most important changes they are bringing is putting decisions affecting our economy back in the hands of each and every one of us rather than in the hands of specialists that most of us can't afford or understand. We've been missing the wisdom of the people doing the actual work, creating actual demand for things to happen, and knowing the resources and problems of which we are unaware.

There are four major changes affecting economics in the last century that dwarf all others. All come from outside of economics, but from real-world, on-the-ground experience. None are fully integrated into our economics yet. They are:

* Examination of economic problems and solutions from a holistic systems perspective, with more meaningful forms of measurement.

* Explicit linkage of life-affirming values and goals with the economic systems needed to attain them.

* Understanding and integrating the ecological and resource underpinnings and interactions of economic systems.

* Acknowledgment of how and how greatly the spiritual dimensions of our existence impact economics.

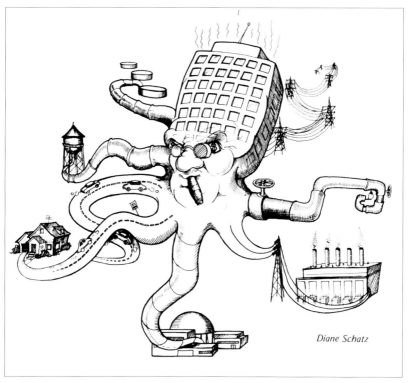

Diane Schatz

All of our actions affect a myriad of other things, whose economic effects we often have ignored. Where we build affects transportation systems and costs. How we build affects need for and cost of water, sewer, electrical, and communications systems. Alternatives to building offer economically significant options.

These new tools represent a reconstitution of economics, giving an unprecedented increase in efficacy. They reveal the most heartening news in a millennium – a one-time opportunity to transform and sustain our planet's ecology, human culture, and all life on Earth.

In looking at these changes, we will be talking little about money. Economics is *not* about money. Money is not real wealth – it is a medium of exchange. It is finance, accounting, and the rules and games to get resources into or out of our own or other people's pockets. We need to look beyond the money transactions to see the real events that are occurring behind the veil of human rules that distort our perceptions and distract our attention. For it is *there* that real change is occurring. The money rules – taxes, subsidies, government regulations, case law – we change daily, to serve the goals we momentarily see as most vital.

What economics *is* about is *resources* – material and energetic; biological and ecological; human, community, and spiritual. It is about work, ingenuity, and time – and about joy. It is about desires and dreams, and the structure of industry and institutions that we use to attain those dreams. Ultimately, it is about wisdom – and it is definitely time to bring that into our balance sheets.

Our economics has been successful at achieving an unprecedented material quality of life for large numbers of people. Yet for most people, that quality of life has been declining since the mid-1970s. And we have been missing potentials for great improvement in effectiveness.

What our economics has been missing is explicit linkage with and consensus on the values it is intended to support and embody. Different goals generate different institutions, products and economic systems. Each framework of economics materializes different dreams and destroys or embodies different values.

Like most things, today's conventional economics has its own internal logic. But whether its tools are appropriate for us to base our whole economy on does not depend on that inner logic, but on its *effectiveness* and ability to attain our goals. When a different tool, such as what we are looking at here, achieves *incomparably* better results, the value of the former approach comes into serious question. A more successful tool, as we shall see, usually helps us also see the blind spots in what we'd been using before, and the reasons it fails to perform as well. The true magnitude of benefits which have been successfully attained through these new tools may initially be hard for many to comprehend. I've included examples that show the simple elements responsible for such benefits.

To keep the focus clearly on the main principles of an economics of wholeness and the process of gaining it, detailed citations and analyses are not included in the body of the text. Please refer to footnoted references for specific studies, citations, and executed projects over the last twenty-five years which give explicit confirmation of the gains achievable through the varied processes.

This book presents things that some economists might consider philosophy, and theory and sociology, and ideas, rather than applied economics. Whatever you may call them, they are not idle musings. They are insights and perspectives gleaned from a now-extensive body of actual implemented projects – constructed and tested buildings, operational and monitored industrial processes, implemented public policies, and lives changed through different working contexts, life goals, and support from community. And they are insights that have been shown to make a difference – a *big* difference. While its content may be many things as well, it *is* unquestionably economics and some of the elements of economics that have wrongfully been neglected in its recent focus on computer modeling.   Economics is about more than how to get rich making widgets. Even the most intransigent will have to come to grips with the success of this new economics – notwithstanding its being developed outside of the realm of professional economists and not from their accepted focus.

Chapter 2
Factor Ten Economics

In 1973, it was considered impossible to achieve order of magnitude (ten-fold or "Factor Ten") improvements in the productivity and resource efficiency of our economic systems. Indeed, it was considered impossible that we could even reduce the rate of *increase* in our energy use per dollar of GNP. Housing costs seemed to be getting unaffordable. Energy costs were soaring, energy use climbing inexorably and high-grade resources being rapidly depleted.

Yet, twenty-five years later, even conventional houses use less than half the energy per square foot than in 1973, and prototypes use 90% less. Toilets use one-quarter the water per flush as in 1973, with toilets available using *no* water. Motor vehicles in 1973 got around 14-mpg. Today, VW is selling a 78-mpg model in Europe and plans a 2003 version with around 235-mpg – a reduction of 94% from 1973.[1] Compact fluorescent light bulbs use only one/fourth the electricity of incandescents, and LED light bulbs due on the market in the next couple of years will drop that another significant factor.

The same dramatic changes are occurring in industry. Between 1981 and 1993, the Louisiana Division of Dow Chemical implemented over a thousand worker-suggested projects to save energy or reduce waste. The projects averaged 204% return on investment, totaling $110 million a year. (These were just incremental shop-floor common-sense improvements, not system-shifts.) Improvements in water use efficiency has already reduced projected world water withdrawals by almost 50%. The Gillette Company has reduced water use in manufacturing razor blades and Paper Mate pens by 90-96%. Armco has reduced water consumption in steel-making by 94%. Similar reduction in material throughputs in industries from carpet-making to office furniture to chemicals are becoming more and more common.[2]

These changes have not come out of a major technological revolution, or from tightening our belts and doing without. These particular examples all involve some changes in technology. (Not all Factor Ten changes do.) But they involve insight and perspectives that find new places and directionality for often quite simple technologies that will achieve radical change.

What these changes have come from is:

* A new conviction, gained from early successes, that we *can* achieve such magnitudes of change.

* Realization that there's a lot of slack in most of our systems because we've tried for years to solve problems by throwing money at them rather than rethinking them.

* Knowledge of the differences between an economics of growth and one of sustainability.

* Seeing that our economics to date has sought only to optimize the particular element it is examining, not the overall system within which it is embedded.

* Understanding that indices used by conventional economics to track success frequently measure the wrong things.

* New ways of thinking outside of the box and looking at economic systems in ways that reveal new possibilities (see Chapter Seven).

Already, world business and governmental leaders are committing to rapid and widespread implementation of Factor Ten economics. The governments of Austria, the Netherlands, and Norway have publicly committed to pursuing Factor Four efficiencies. The European Union has endorsed the concept as the new paradigm for sustainable development. Austria, Sweden, and OECD environment ministers have urged the adoption of Factor Ten goals, as have the World Business Council for Sustainable Development and the United Nations Environment Program (UNEP). Leading corporations worldwide are adopting it as a powerful strategy to gain competitive advantage.[3]

How did we get from there to here, and what more can we expect in the future? As one of the individuals and organizations involved in the development of Factor Ten economics,[4] I can tell part of the story.

In 1973, I was becoming more and more concerned with our culture's voracious and rapidly growing appetites for material resources, energy, and land. These were all limited and non-renewable resources. With then-existing trends, we would begin to run out in a few decades, even without making their benefits available to the other 95% of the world's population. The only alternative presented us was the looming specter of nuclear power with its Faustian twin, nuclear war. Was there a way to escape this voracious consumption and the destruction it causes; to live more lightly, simply, and happily?

I knew that wonderful, sophisticated, and wise cultures have existed everywhere on the planet with much less impact on resources. I knew also that we needed to find an answer that worked not just for us, but for *all* of the world. We were only beginning to put together the requisites for sustainability, but best estimates were that the U.S. would have to reduce our material and energy consumption by at least 80% to reach a level sustainable for the entire planet. That was daunting. *Reducing* our energy use by 80%, when it currently was *increasing* by at least 10% per year.

It was worth a try. Trained as an architect, I knew that our buildings were connected with major parts of our energy use, so I had a place to start. We also were building one of the very first regionally self-reliant demonstration houses in one of the courses I was teaching at the university, so we had relatively good information on some alternatives.

With the proverbial back of an envelope, I started to look at our homes, and how we could avoid or reduce energy use in heating, cooling, lighting, cooking, clothes washing, bathrooms, appliances, the materials used in building the house, the energy consumed by automobiles getting us from our home to other places, the cycle of nutrients and energy in our food. The results? Earth-shattering:

> *"It is possible today, without hardship, to reduce the energy consumption of our society by 90%, and live happily on less than one-tenth of the energy we now use, while at the same time enriching our freedom, our enjoyment, and our lives."*[5]

The surprising bonus was that our lives would likely be better – this dramatic shift didn't mean going back to the cave. This one study established the possibility of Factor Ten economics, laid out the principles of finding similar solutions in other parts of our economy, and gave a clear example of its application.

The demonstration house we were building, Project Ouroboros,[6] took this new energy-economics instantly from theory to action in Minnesota's rugged climate. Compost toilets, active and passive solar heating, greenhouses, night window insulation, super-insulation, earth-berm construction, wind electricity, recycled materials, sod roofs were all part of the equation. What they showed was the old ecological truism, *"The whole is greater than the sum of the parts."* Putting the right pieces together reduced *need* for energy enough that it *could* be met with renewable energies. And this wasn't theory – people could see and touch all the systems in operation. This was real.

Since the Ouroboros Project (in construction in 1973, above) this design of residential construction has become a regional pattern, with a dozen or more visible from a single road crossing Minnesota. Solar collectors still under night snow, above right; south windows below; sod roof out of sight, above left.

In October, 1973, I quietly released a paper, *"Living Lightly: Energy Conservation in Housing,"* which summarized the study and the demonstration house (still in construction), and showed how the U.S. could reduce energy use by a phenomenal 90% while simultaneously *improving* quality of life. The piece spread like wildfire across the country in dog-eared photocopies, and was reprinted by organization after organization.[7] People no longer thought the idea was crazy. *Living Lightly* had freed our mind-set and got us really looking at what we *could* do. The impossible was now possible. We were on our way.

We knew we could do Factor Ten in energy, and in housing, but how about industry, public institutions, and looking at other resource use in economics? It turned out that the hardest part was the first step. The rest was just doing it. We were soon seeing the blindingly obvious I'd first found in *Living Lightly* everywhere:

> *"Durability pays!"* We don't need any fancy technology to make what we build ten times more productive. We just need to build our automobiles and houses and schools and churches to last! A building that lasts 200 years is already a Factor Ten building for *all* the resources put into its making, compared to one built to last only twenty years.

> *"Don't solve problems, avoid them!"* It is always simpler to avoid product packaging than to recycle it, to keep PCB's out of products than to clean up hazardous spills, to avoid air leakage out of a house than to provide make-up heat for what is lost through leakage.

> *"Live simply, work less!"* No matter how hard we work, the money seems to go out as fast as it comes in. What we can do with the freedom of our time from working less is often far more rewarding than what we would spend money on from working more.

> *"Stop tourism – make where we are paradise!"* Live near where we work, make our communities so wonderful that we want to spend our vacations at home rather than consuming fuel to travel far away.

> *"Public and private expenditures on health services, transportation, education, or defense are definitely costs, but not necessarily a measure of benefit received!"* Seems we shouldn't have to need this reminder, but all too frequently we equate expenditure on a new car or a new highway or hospital or sewage system as an improvement or benefit, rather than asking what had gotten worse about where we were so we needed to get away from it, or what made so many more people sick and needing a new hospital.

This should have been obvious, except we were so used to looking at the fine print of conventional economics that we couldn't look past the twenty year depreciation on a building.

Living Lightly dealt with energy use. But as further studies were done, the tools developed in *Living Lightly* and the conviction that we could find order-of-magnitude improvements in our ways of doing things were applied successfully where the economic resources involved were not primarily energy.

The next application of the Factor Ten principles and perspectives developed in *Living Lightly* unexpectedly turned out to be in government policy. The 1973-4 "Arab Oil Crisis" hit the State of Oregon a devastating blow, and an urgent call came from Governor Tom McCall's office for assistance in developing energy policy to deal with the crisis. Nobody else, it seemed, had conceived of dramatic reduction in energy use being possible or, even more, having *positive* benefits. Three months after *Living Lightly* was published, I was working in the Governor's Office on energy policy.

Three papers we prepared in the Governor's Office of Energy Research and Planning (OERP) stand out for their dramatic advance in our perspectives of dealing with managing our material and energy resources and the interesting interactions between Howard Odum's *net* energy concepts, costs of obtaining all material and energy resources, and their impact on inflation: *"Cosmic Economics," "Emerging Energy Policy Principles,"* and *"Independence?"*[8]

These papers, whose advice is still well taken today, demonstrate the value of comprehensive understanding of the economic resource context of our governmental policies. *"Independence?"* states:

Our only realistic options for resolving our energy problems are to:

* Use remaining depletable energy reserves to move toward use of safe and continuously available energy, such as solar energy.

* Increase utilization of human skills and effort to make possible lower overall energy use. [This meant *both* using employment rather than energy, and using ingenuity to figure out efficiency strategies.]

* Recognize and increase the utilization of the free work of natural systems, such as allowing natural lands to perform tertiary treatment of sewage.

* Reduce our demands to levels which can extend the life of our reserves and which can be sustained by future energy budgets.

* Store sufficient portions of our proven energy reserves for emergency use to insure the stability and soundness of our society.

* Earmark energy tax revenues to assist all people to meet basic human needs during the transition to permanently sustainable levels of energy consumption.

Particularly when dealing with depletable energy resources which conventional economics valued at cost of obtaining rather than cost of replacement, these perspectives were pioneering in establishing appropriate policy directions. One-third of our energy has come from renewable sources, two-thirds from fossil fuels. Factor Ten improvements in resource productivity shift our use to magnitudes which can be supplied largely through renewable resources.

In the fall of 1975, after McCall left office, Lane deMoll and I moved to Portland to join friends Lee and Steve Johnson in publishing *RAIN Magazine*, which became a model for networking information to leverage change, further develop principles and applications of the new economics, and for empowering decentralized local initiatives. The magazine acted as a forum for further exploring many of the issues of the new economics – the interplay of values, directionality of technology, politics, energy, community organization. People in the RAIN network were, and are, doers – and soon there was a whole network of people working with implementing the new perspectives in diverse areas.

The first dramatic impact on the normal business world occurred in 1975-6 when Seattle City Light, a municipal electric utility in Washington State, commissioned a study on energy conservation and renewable energy sources. (This was the era when the accepted industry and government wisdom was to join Washington Public Power Supply System's pending leap into financial disaster with an expansive and unaffordable program of nuclear power development.)

Part of the study fell to friends in the RAIN network from Ecotope Group in Seattle. Following through on our systems perspectives, they put hard numbers on some interesting options. Tremors ran through the Seattle business world when SCL released the study,[9] unequivocally showing that the utility would make more money *giv-*

ing away insulation to homeowners than building *any* new source of electricity. This was not business as usual. It broke all the rules of economic common sense. *Making* money by *giving away* product?

When the dust settled, a whole nest of new analytical concepts had transformed the entire US electrical utility industry, and a new systems-based approach to economic analysis had gained credibility. Demand reduction and management (DSM), without reducing delivered benefit, *was* far cheaper than new electricity production. A whole new "least cost" policy began to govern public utilities and regulated private ones throughout the country.[10] Systemic analysis of overall cost and benefits, and purchase of "least-cost" power – which usually meant efficiency improvements rather than new energy production – became standard. Insulating houses was much cheaper than heating houses that lack insulation. Building codes were quickly revised to ensure obtaining those benefits in all new construction and retrofits.

Another step occurred in 1981, when the State of California held an *Affordable Housing Competition* to find solutions to the apparent increasing unaffordability of housing. The first thing I found out in the top-award-winning study I did was that the competition was based on an assumption that *construction* costs were making housing unaffordable, and that "new technologies" or skimping on quality were the expected answers.

It turned out that housing hadn't gotten significantly more expensive. Growing income disparity is what was making housing unaffordable. Nobody had ever looked at what *did* make up the overall costs that a family pays for housing over their lifetime. When I did assemble that information, the actual costs that overshadowed all others, including construction, were the costs of *energy* to operate the house and *financing* costs that were paid over a family's or a building's life! Some improvements in construction techniques and costs could be gained, of course, but they were irrelevant compared to the magnitude of energy and mortgage expenditures and potential for savings in those areas.

Seeing what constituted the true costs of housing made it easy to focus on developing innovative ways to avoid, eliminate, or reduce financing costs; dramatically increase durability and energy efficiency; reduce selling costs; and see how they could interact to create momentous savings. Financing, selling and durability costs proved to be as amenable to Factor Ten savings as energy costs had in the *Living Lightly* study. Ways were developed again to reduce housing costs by an equally unbelievable 75-90%.[11]

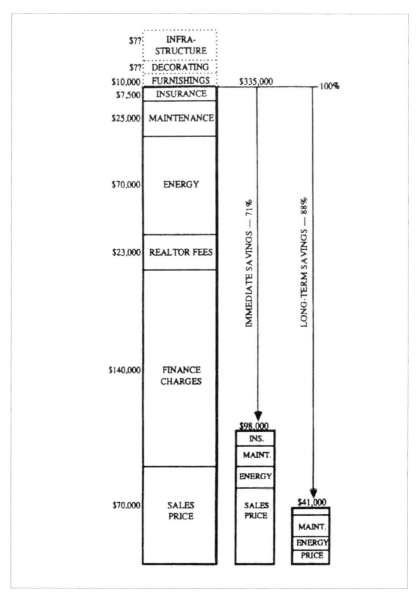

Operating energy and finance charges are the dominant lifetime costs of owning a house. Focusing on strategies to reduce those costs are more effective than minimizing original construction costs.

— From "Hidden Costs of Housing"

Later studies and projects I have done examining other elements of our economic system and expanding the perspectives of Factor Ten economics will be discussed elsewhere in this volume.[12]

By now it was clear that we had the tools and perspectives to bring massive change and magnitude improvement in the effectiveness of virtually any human activity that we examined. Charles Komonoff, Amory Lovins and others were beginning to do wonderful things in the area of energy – demanding full costing of energy alternatives such as nuclear power whose true costs and massive government subsidies were being ignored, and demonstrating the multiple savings and benefits of energy efficiency and renewable energy which were being ignored in most policy decisions. I was free to turn my attention to developing other elements of the new economics.

Application of the Factor Ten principles expanded rapidly over the next decade, with proven success in academic analysis, industrial implementation, government policy, and private actions. In the fall of 1994, the concept took a giant leap forward with the gathering in Carnoules, France, of a group of government officials, economists, scientists and business people called by the Wuppertal Institute in Germany. This meeting resulted in publishing of the *Carnoules Declaration*, calling for an order-of-magnitude leap in resource productivity to reverse the growing ecological and social damage of materials and energy use from human activity. As a result of that meeting, Europe has taken the leadership in business application and governmental policy, and become the proving ground for its technical application.

Ernst von Weizsächer, Amory and L. Hunter Lovins' *Factor Four*, 1997; and Paul Hawken, Amory and L. Hunter Lovins' *Natural Capitalism*, 1999, cover this story, giving innumerable examples and case studies of revolutionizing energy, material, and transportation productivity as irrefutable demonstration of its successful use in a wide spectrum of application. Examples include super-appliances and office equipment that use 75-90% less energy; houses and offices in different climates that require virtually no outside energy to operate; polycultural and bio-intensive farming; water efficiency in manufacturing, residences, and agriculture; high resource-productivity in industrial processes, quadrupling the capacity of existing railways, and reducing the need for commuting through transit-oriented development.

Development of the Hypercar, a revolutionary redesign of the automobile from the ground up to give order-of-magnitude improvement in energy and material use is a wonderful case-in-point. Begun in 1991 at the Rocky Mountain Institute, and being brought from theory into production by Hypercar, Inc., the project represents the first clean-slate redesign of the automobile in a century. Starting with the realization that less than one percent of the energy in the fuel has actually been used to move the occupants around, the project has sought three main goals:

 * 50-65% reduction in vehicle weight that had to be moved around, while increasing occupant safety, through use of high-strength composites and sophisticated crash-safe design. Use of iron and steel would be reduced about 92%.

 * 30-40% reduction in rolling resistance from air and tires.

 * Radical improvement in fuel use efficiency through hybrid-electric propulsion. Combined with lower weight and rolling resistance, the goal for fuel efficiency was 150-200mpg.

© 2000 Hypercar, Inc.

Courtesy Hypercar, Inc.

Hybrid gas-electric propelled, SUV capacity, Hypercar vehicle with potential 100-200 mpg fuel economy and easily recyclable components.

 Redesign also sought major simplification in the number of parts to assemble, and in the recyclability of the completed vehicle. Body design was simplified to 14 major and 62 total components vs. 250-300 in a conventional vehicle (a 75-80% reduction). Heat gain into the vehicle was reduced 80% to cut air-conditioning needs, and sidestick controls substituted for steering wheels, gearshifts, brakes, and clutches to simplify controls and passenger compartment design. Integrated digital control systems have been developed to simplify the mass of wiring inside the vehicle.

The current Hypercar prototype is fuel-cell operated, with projected fuel economies of the first design being equivalent to 99mpg, with expectations of double that in later models. The design is consistent with a 200,000 mile warranty.[13]

The changes coming about through Factor Ten economics are radical, and are achieving the most significant change in economic productivity in the last century. But somehow there seemed to be more to the picture. It kept nagging at me that we were missing some important limitations and opportunities.

One of the pieces was obvious. We had passed the difficult beginning of the bell-curve – where we had figured out that something was wrong, something better was possible, and how to achieve it. Now we were on the lovely bulge of the curve where everything seemed easy. Huge gains were lying around everywhere, just waiting to be gathered in. The future looked rosy. As always, we were picking the juicy low-hanging fruit, forgetting that soon there would only be hard-to-get ones left:

* *Factor Ten gains are likely to become harder and harder to obtain, when efficiency of systems and meta-systems have been upgraded through previous Factor Ten actions.*

Factor Ten improvements are possible today for several reasons:

* Inefficiencies caused by gaps and omissions in our past economic thinking and measurement.

* New technologies and insights permitting higher resource effectiveness.

* Poorly and piecemeal conceived, organized and operated institutions and industrial processes.

There is no certainty of ongoing major improvements once impacts of these new perspectives are gained:

* *In the big picture, Factor Ten gains may be a one-shot shift in thinking (though increasing productivity 1000% isn't to be sneezed at).*

Another issue that has to be dealt with is that true aggregate savings are slippery and often illusory. *Every dollar we save is usually spent on something else.* It doesn't matter whether savings come from reduced energy use in a building, institutional change, or other Factor Ten productivity gains. The savings are almost invariably spent on vacations, a new car, an education, or just paying the bills. As those same dollars ripple around the economy – just purchasing *different* things – they end up using up similar amounts of energy and resources as before.[14]   There seem to be only a few apparent anomalies:

> * Converting those savings to *freed time* – through working less, earning less, and therefore spending less. This *does* achieve aggregate reduction in resource use.

> * Using those savings for different beneficiaries and goals, such as improving the well-being of the less wealthy. This doesn't reduce resource use, but changes the beneficiaries and makes the poor less likely to be a cost, or resource burden, to society in the future.

> * Investing those savings in renewable resources, ecosystem restoration, and further resource productivity. This can lead to more enduring benefits.

After working for twenty-five years to cut in half the use of wood in a building (and equivalently the ecological impact of logging) we find that, because of growth in population and second homes, we're now cutting *twice* as many trees to build twice as many, twice as large houses.

Changes in resource productivity can produce enduring reduction in resource use – <u>only</u> if growth is stabilized. Factor Ten changes resulting in <u>financial</u> savings only result in a displacement to other economic activities, unless we work less or otherwise reduce our economic activity.

And there is a tricky catch to order-of-magnitude changes:

Each <u>subsequent</u> order-of-magnitude change gives an order-of-magnitude <u>less</u> change than the previous.

The first Factor Ten change reduces costs or resource use by 90%. The second Factor Ten change saves 90% of the *remaining* 10%, but that is only a *9%* (not 90%) change from the *original*. And changes in a larger system may lose or duplicate earlier gains made in the subsystems. Not only are subsequent changes likely to be harder to obtain, but each can only achieve an order-of-magnitude *less* improvement than the last.

There is no assurance that Factor Ten changes can continue to be obtained over a long period or at presently achievable magnitudes. If they aren't, there are deeper questions we need to address, which will be discussed in Chapter Six. Particularly if they are a one-shot deal (still an immense accomplishment) there are related aspects we need to consider. We'll take a look at those in later chapters.

Factor Ten economics achieves the magnitude of improvements it does by looking at things as a "whole" as well as examining the individual parts that make up the whole, and their cross-effects. Often an improvement in one of the parts that is not cost-effective in itself can make possible elimination of another whole element, or through savings created in connected systems. (For example: increasing the insulation level of a building to the point where the entire heating system can be eliminated; improving energy efficiency of equipment in a building to the point where the occupancy heat load is reduced enough to totally eliminate the need for air conditioning; or intermixing home and workplaces in a city to avoid need for freeways to commute long distances to work.) In Chapter Seven, we'll look at successful strategies that can be applied in other situations.

Factor Ten economics as most widely applied today deals centrally with resource productivity. But that is only one piece of the story. When combined with the perspectives in the following chapters, it can produce order-of-magnitude improvements in financial performance, institutional effectivness, and in the achievement of our personal and societal goals. The issues in those areas are usually perceptual rather than technological, and gains can be achieved with equal or greater ease. Combined with Factor Ten resource productivity gains, they open unprecedented opportunities for our future.

Factor Ten gains are achievable in several very different dimensions of our economy. Almost any analysis we do in the real world results in an apparent jumble of new benefits. For simplicity's sake, we can lump those gains into four categories, and use those to check when summarizing impacts and to see where other dimensions of benefit might be obtained:

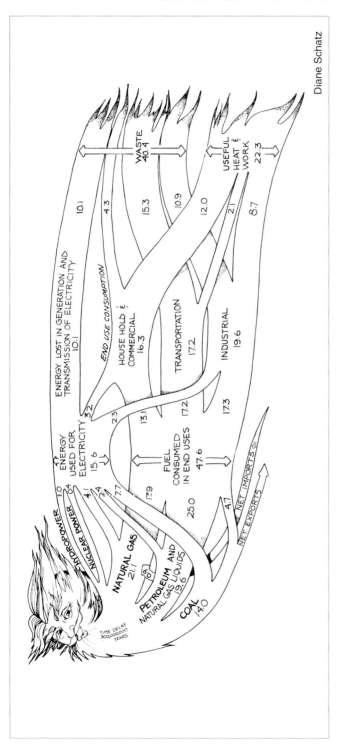

Diane Schatz

Mapping overall energy flows through a region (here the State of Oregon) from original sources through conversion to other forms of energy, its end uses, and losses involved in each area gives perspective where major opportunities for improvement in productivity might be possible.
— from TRANSITION

* *Resource productivity gains* – using less energy to heat a house or materials to construct a building. Often requires new technologies, and varies dramatically as to whether initial financial costs are greater or less. Direct benefits are reduced production, consumption, depletion, and competition for resources; ecological impacts; expenditures on resources. Secondary benefits are often in the area of avoided social conflicts, impacts on others, future financial costs.

* *Institutional and financial performance gains* – These gains involve finding new patterns and processes to achieve a similar end product. Redesigning the automobile to eliminate 80% of the parts; lengthening timber harvest rotations to reduce the work of logging, planting, thinning, and managing by 75%; direct marketing to reduce warehousing, distribution, and retail sales costs. Primary benefits are often financial, with secondary resource productivity and well-being benefits.

* *Personal and social well-being gains* – This often involves finding non-material ways to more effectively achieve our real goals and quality of life. Clarity, not technology, is usually most central. More durable products, shorter work weeks, more free time, rather than producing and consuming more unneeded things. Asking basic questions about equity, costs of growth or debt. Displacement of making "things" gives secondary reduction in resource needs. Primary benefits are psychological, emotional, spiritual; happiness, accomplishment, esteem. Secondary benefits are resource and financial.

* *Planetary health and goals gains* – Impacts of our actions on the total web of life. Toilets that use less water reduce water purification and distribution costs, sewage processing costs, costs of obtaining new water supplies, conflicts over different uses of limited water supplies, aquatic health. Living near our work reduces need for transportation, saves commuting time, often brings us closer to other people, lessens pollution and stress, frees us to connect more deeply with others. Primary impacts are overall social and ecological effectiveness, with secondary benefits being financial, emotional, and resource-related.

Order-of-magnitude lower resource need, increased material goods and services, improved quality of life, less ecological impact, and more meaningful goals to our lives and society are worthy of attention. All can be achieved together through layering of different Factor Ten strategies and actions.

Order-of-magnitude gains are simultaneously possible in ALL these dimensions, transforming our lives far more deeply than mere efficient production of more goods.

PARTS AND WHOLES

Approaching things from a systems perspective gives vital insights on wise allocation of resources. Conventionally, we view things in isolation and try to optimize their costs and benefits. For a building, we may try to obtain a certain performance and longevity at lowest cost. As we expand our perspective from initial cost to lifecycle cost, including the committments initial construction makes for 50 to 100 years of energy use, transportation, and maintenance over the life of the building, what is wise changes. Greater initial investment, for insulation, efficient heating and lighting systems, or daylighting can save many times their cost over the life of the building.

But when we broaden our perspective a bit further, and consider not just the building in isolation, but its contribution to the effectiveness of the institution it houses, we discover that optimizing the cost of the embedded system (here the building) rather than the embracing system (the institution it houses) can be counterproductive. I showed in 1976, for the California State Architect, that building construction and operation makes up only a small fraction of overall institutional costs as an operating entity. Relatively large changes in building costs that produce even small changes in employee productivity, for example, can produce immense return on investment.[15] A building that produced only 6% productivity increase could cost four times as much and still be a wise investment. A building owner needs to look at employee turnover rates, absenteeism rates, and "goof-off" and "goof-up" rates, and how

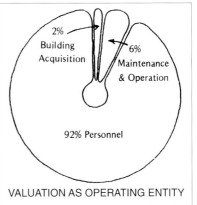

2%
Building Acquisition

6%
Maintenance & Operation

92% Personnel

VALUATION AS OPERATING ENTITY

they can be improved by workplaces that improve their emotional, spiritual, and physical health. Subsequent evaluations of "green offices" has confirmed that they can be extremely profitable investments, through improving worker productivity.[16] What benefits us most is optimizing the *greater* system, not the subsystem.

---

[1] RMI Solutions Newsletter, Spring 2001.

[2] FACTOR FOUR, Ernst von Weizsäcker, Amory and L. Hunter Lovins, Earthscan, 1997.

[3] NATURAL CAPITALISM, Paul Hawken, Amory and L. Hunter Lovins, Little, Brown & Company, 1999.

[4] The others who I know were centrally involved were Amory Lovins' Rocky Mountain Institute, and Ernst von Weizsäcker's Wuppertal Institute in Germany.

[5] LIVING LIGHTLY: Energy Conservation in Housing, Tom Bender, October 1973.

[6] See cover article, POPULAR SCIENCE, Dec. 1975.

[7] Including RAIN Magazine, State of Oregon Governor's Office, Evergreen College, University of Minnesota, and other university and environmental programs.

[8] *"Cosmic Economics," "Emerging Energy Policy Principles,"* and *"Independence?,"* Joel Schatz and Tom Bender, Governor's Office, State of Oregon, 1974.

[9] ENERGY 1990 STUDY, Initial Report (7 volumes), prepared for the City of Seattle Department of Lighting (now Seattle City Light), by a consultant team headed by NW Environmental Technology Laboratories, Inc., with assistance from Mathematical Sciences, Inc., and Energy, Inc., 1976.

[10] LEAST-COST ENERGY PLANNING, Roger L. Sant, 1974.

[11] See *"Hidden Costs of Housing"*, Tom Bender, RAIN Magazine, Mar/Apr 1984. Reprinted in UTNE READER, Summer 1984; SUN TIMES, Nov/Dec 1984; ALTERNATIVE PRESS ANNUAL, 1984.

[12] See bibliography for subsequent studies and articles and their primary focus.

[13] See <www.hypercar.org>; Rocky Mountain Institute Newsletter and publications, <www.rmi.org>.

[14] Shifts from energy-intensive to less energy intensive expenditures *do* reduce energy use, but by only the net difference. Some alternatives, such as vacations, can be *more* energy-intensive. And second-tier expenditures narrow the gap further. See *"Eco-building II,"* Tom Bender, ENVIRONMENTAL BUILDING NEWS, July 1996; IN CONTEXT, July 1996.

[15] *BUILDING VALUE*, Tom Bender. Office of California State Architect, 1976.

[16] *GREENING THE BUILDING AND THE BOTTOM LINE*, Joseph Romm and William Browning, Rocky Mountain Institute, 1994.

Chapter 3
Qualities, Goals, and Values

Interestingly, Factor Ten economics achieves by far its greatest gains when it connects up with aspects of our lives previously considered unworthy of inclusion in economic analyses. Among them are values and non-material goals; ecology, material and energy resources; chi energy and the sacred – which we'll look at in subsequent chapters. These are all "qualitative" factors resistant to quantification, but playing vital roles in our lives.

QUALITIES

There are two very divergent definitions of "qualitative" in use today. The first, widely used in economics, is *"subtle differences not significant enough to be quantified or counted."* A quilt, vs. *the* quilt your grandmother made. If you can't quantify the differences, forget it, it's not worth dealing with. The second definition is *"characteristics of essential being that are sufficiently different that two things aren't comparable."* Apples and bricks. You can't quantify comparisons because the yardsticks are totally different. In one, the differences are too *insubstantial* to deal with; in the other the differences are *too substantial* to have common basis for comparison. Indistinguishable vs. incomparable.

We are dealing centrally in economics of wholeness with elements that are incomparable, but essential, and which must be incorporated at a root level into our decisions, and therefore our economics.

The role of economics is to help <u>clarify</u>, not quantify, our consideration of alternatives.

One of the essential elements that economics of wholeness is bringing back into our decision-making processes, is the addressing of major and elemental differences that *neither can <u>nor need to be</u> quantified*. Either we're looking at work as something to be minimized, automated, simplified to the point of interchangeability; or we're looking at work as an essential attribute contributing vital things to our lives.

A similar disparity has arisen in our use of the word "count." Its conventional meaning in economics is "ascertaining the number of elements in a group." Equally or more importantly, however, it also means "to possess value, to esteem, or to judge." We need to use both of its meanings in economics – learning to count what *really* counts – or learning to measure and esteem what truly possesses value. What is important in our lives?

The nice thing analytically is that *we don't need a lot of numbers when everything adds up in the same direction.* Quantitative analysis is *only* necessary where the differences between options are *insignificant* enough to be only quantitative.

The ignoring of core qualitative elements of our lives by conventional economics understandably has lead to significant "inefficiencies." Those economic costs can be addressed by bringing such core elements back into our decisions and actions. We can see now that by the latter part of the 20th century, those inefficiencies had grown to order-of-magnitude size, making unquestionable the benefits of returning a "qualitative" nucleus to economics which addresses proper resolution of fundamental "qualitative" differences.

Quantification remains a valuable tool for fine-tuning and for testing assumptions and alternatives in limited situations. Outdated pricing structures that do not reflect real costs; ideological beliefs that large through-puts of materials, energy, and money necessarily contribute to social or personal well-being; tax and financial structures that support special interests and waste of resources; and split incentives that discourage design and use of efficient products make any comparisons unrealistic. Until we reflect the richness and interactiveness of the real world in our analyses, no economics can provide either qualitative or quantitatively reliable and realistic information.

IMMEASURABLE WEALTH

Most of our *real* wealth is composed of these very same intangibles. Experiencing love and being loved, feeling of value to others, knowing we have something to contribute. Friendship, peace, security, health, well-being, adventure, joy, passion, spirit. Meaningfulness and purpose of our life, growth, fullness, experience, successful meeting of challenges, knowledge and expansion of our own capabilities. Helping others, being able to create and give, the excitement of exploring worlds and wisdom beyond just that of human life, joining with others into richer untouched possibilities.

Intangible wealth is not alone in being ignored by our existing economic tools. Another significant element of our material wealth is *durable* wealth – potentially long-lived vehicles, buildings, roads, or water systems. A good measure of our skewed economic accounting is that we customarily discount virtually all future benefits of long-lived goods. The true continuing benefit of durable goods so far outweighs those of ephemeral, or consumable, goods that competent economic tools would have us investing heavily in such infrastructure.

A third realm of wealth that doesn't play by the rules is that of *intellectual* wealth. Sometimes costly to obtain, atrophies without use, costs virtually nothing to share, and using it often creates more. Similarly, the work of natural systems, volunteer work and that done in the home rarely get proper weight in the making of decisions.

Our real "limits to growth" are not material supply limits, but the limits of our <u>perceptions</u> blocking us from seeing far greater potentials available in non-material and unquantifiable aspects of our lives. The interesting and favorable "economic" benefits of a stable-state society are also turning out to be outpaced by the even greater rewards they make possible in non-economic dimensions of our lives.

Past a certain point, our needs, wants, and desires are better met by means other than material goods. Limits of material *satisfaction* are also more important than the limits of material production. Beyond a certain level of food, clothing and shelter, our real interests lie in gaining wisdom, respect, status, security, enjoyment, and cultivation of our minds, bodies, and spirits, and community. All of which have little correlation with material wealth.

TRANSCENDING PROBLEMS

Even our most intractable problems are solvable. They frequently require a process of *surmounting* or *transcending* the apparently mutually exclusive viewpoints that have arisen from each of our faceted fields of personal experience and trained beliefs. That process of transcendence usually involves expanding our experience to include an overarching third element. Broadening our perspective allows us to see opposites as *complementary dualities* – essential polarizations of unity (as in the Chinese *yin/yang*) – which are encompassed and catalyzed into an essential whole.

According to E.F. Schumacher, every society needs both stability *and* change, tradition *and* innovation, public interest *and* private interest, planning *and* laissez-faire, order *and* freedom, growth *and* decay.[0] Every society's health depends on the simultaneous pursuit of apparently mutually opposed activities or aims. The tension between these pairs of opposites that permeate everything we do is a vital aspect of life. That tension, to be fruitful, requires a transcendence – in which higher forces such as love, compassion, understanding, and empathy become available as regular and reliable resources to create a dynamic unity out of the opposed forces.

Schumacher also observed that there are four different fields of experience that create our awareness of our world:

* Awareness of what is happening in our own inner world.

* Awareness of what is happening in the inner world of others, or of other life.

* Knowing how we appear to others.

* Observing how others appear to us.

Importantly, each of these fields is accessed by different means. We can directly access our invisible inner world and how others appear to us. Yet what we see can be very different from what others see. We frequently perceive and judge ourselves by our *intentions*, while others see and judge us more by our *actions*. There is often no way we can directly compare our experience of love, pain, or anger to that of others. And what we track and pay attention to in the world around us varies radically depending on our values, sensitivities, and inner knowledge.

The other two fields of knowing we cannot access directly at all. They involve putting ourselves in others' shoes and the difficult communication of inner knowledge through symbols. It is often difficult to convert inner experience into communicable symbols, and we can't foresee how those symbols will be experienced internally by others. They are resistant to any attempts at quantification and prediction, as they involve living, changing natures; predictability belongs only to the fixed nature of less complex levels of being.

As we move from the material world of minerals, physics, and chemistry to the plant, animal, and human world, there is an intensification of life, consciousness and self-awareness. Quickly, the dynamic nature of those aspects of life overshadow the fixed, predictable, and quantifiable aspects that are amenable to the "scientific" tools we have used. As that complexity increases, probing into the levels of existence where these things arise and interact, become essential to our awareness and action. In terms of economics, it may mean admitting we can't always anticipate the needs of others. It might be wise by starting by giving *them* control of goals and means of attaining the ones *they* feel most important.

To experience the world whole requires a unity of knowing – the integration and balance of these four fields of knowledge gained through appropriate processes. That unity is destroyed if one or more fields are uncultivated or examined with instruments or methods applicable only to other fields. The method used must correspond to the field studied. Our "logical" sciences only apply to the fourth field: observing the appearances of how the world looks to us. Self-knowledge, essential both for knowing our inner world and for translating communications of other's inner worlds, must be balanced by the often different knowledge of how we appear to others. Social knowledge, vital for indirectly accessible knowledge, requires self-knowledge as a basis. An economics of wholeness must be openly structured enough to be based on different knowing of our world.

GOALS

Our deepest goals are rarely material, nor economic:

* Experiencing love and being loved, feeling of value to others, knowing we have something to contribute.

* Friendship, peace, security, health, well-being, adventure, joy, passion, spirit.

* Meaningfulness and purpose of our life, growth, fullness, experience, successful meeting of challenges, knowledge and expansion of our own capabilities.

* Helping others, being able to create and give, the excitement of exploring worlds and wisdom beyond just that of human life, joining with others into richer untouched possibilities.

All are hard to quantify or to buy. All have to come from within. We achieve them more directly by focusing our personal actions, governmental policy, and economic indicators to eliminate discord and to align our lives to those goals. Each of our everyday actions contribute to and make possible all of these goals. It is through them that our inner and outer growth occurs, and our connection with others and with other life. The values those daily actions are based on inalterably makes goals we seek possible or unachievable.

Our goal is Life . . .
– experiencing its fullest and most awesome possibilities.
– healthy and continuing undiminished by our actions.
– the life of all of Creation, not just ourselves.

Our goal is Liberty . . .
– for us and for others.
– for the future as well as now.
– within the law of nature.

Our goal is the Pursuit of Happiness . . .
– the happiness of being able to love people, with all their quirks and oddities.
– the happiness of being able to love our places, our things, the many-legged and winged and rooted peoples.

– being able to love the earth, the sun, the wind and rain, in
    their difficult as well as welcome times.
– being able to love ourselves.
– being able to love the happiness of others.
– being able to love the happiness of pursuit, or the "doing,"
    as much as the end itself.
– being able to love these indivisibly, not as things apart.

Keep these goals clear and present, for they will illuminate the right
path among often seductive choices.

>The goal is not wealth, power, or progress.
>For the joy in these is fleeting.
>
>The goal is not education,
>or science, or technology, or comfort,
>or security or health.
>These are means, at best –
>things as often to be given up as gained
>to reach things of greater import.

*Our rewards from life come in measure to <u>what</u> we seek and <u>how</u> we
seek it.*

VALUES

    Economics is not, and cannot be, a science separate and unto
itself. It is never value-free. The values it serves may be assumed,
hidden, or unaware. But every value system brings into being dis-
tinctly different economic systems, and every economic system embodies or destroys very specific and distinct systems of values. Any
discussion of economics which does not acknowledge the values it
serves is intentionally or unintentionally omitting some of the most
crucial elements to its success.

    The period we have just gone through of supposedly "value-
free" economics and culture has been vital. It has forced us to clearly
experience the results of absence of certain values and to reforge a deep
understanding of their purpose and importance to us. It has allowed
us to explore new kinds of technologies, social and political organization, and assumptions about our world. From testing our past assumptions, and through being able to repeat evolutionary dead ends that

nature has already abandoned, we have the opportunity to come to a closer understanding of the real possibilities and limitations of our world. Such understanding can give us greater and more precisely defined freedom and more thorough understanding of what we can and should do and not do.

Value distinctions seem ephemeral when considered beside profit and loss statements, yet profit and loss statements hold little meaning when viewed from the next generation, or when viewed beside the loss of the irreplaceable physical realities upon which the continuing support of our lives must depend. Values are really a complex and compact depository of survival wisdom – expressions of those feelings, attitudes, actions, and relationships we have found to be most supportive of our well being within certain physical realities.

SIX PILLARS OF SUCCESS[1]
There are only a few principles or root values that underlie an enduring society:

* Equity
* Security
* Sustainability
* Responsibility
* Giving
* Sacredness

Together, they ensure the well-being of all life, and the marshaling of our actions and dreams effectively to achieve the best for all. They encompass the restoration of health to our lives:

EQUITY:
* To ensure that all people have equitable access to and share of wealth, health, income, security, education, opportunity, respect, political power, and fulfilling work.

* To ensure that all life has the scope to ensure well-being and development of innate capabilities.

SECURITY:
* To remove the imbalances of power, self-esteem, opportunity, resource access, and emotional health which form the base of fear and insecurity.

* To realize that biosystem health, a lasting supply of world resources, and the capabilities of human and global systems – not material consumption rates – constitute our real wealth. To act to ensure and improve the health and capabilities of these resources.

SUSTAINABILITY:
* To stabilize and restore population to long term supportable levels commensurate with the well-being of all life.

* To draw materials and energy only from renewable sources and at sustainable rates.

* To work within those energy and material use levels to both improve our non-material quality of life and more effectively provide for our material needs.

RESPONSIBILITY:
* To enact full ecological analysis to ensure public knowledge of the true costs of our actions.

* To live within our sustainable incomes, not take from future generations and other life, and to ensure them undiminished opportunity for fulfillment.

* To ensure that all industrial producers assume eternal responsibility for the products and byproducts they create.

* To protect and preserve farm, forest, aquatic, and other natural resources.

* To protect natural, cultural and spiritual resources until all jurisdictions restore and enhance their own to levels which meet the needs of their populations.

GIVING:
* To acknowledge the primacy of non-material rewards in personal and community health and develop giving-based principles of interaction which honor the contribution of all life to what we hold of value.

* To replace our violent forms of obtaining food and resources with ones which are based on consensus and fulfilling the needs of all parties.

* To ensure all have roles in the community which offer meaningful self-esteem, mutual respect, and being of value to the community of all life.

SACREDNESS:

* To acknowledge that our greatest cultural problems are at root diseases of the spirit. To act to improve the spiritual, mental, psychological and communal dimensions of our real wealth and their expression in our communities.

* To seek the wisdom and connectedness to restore well-being to all of Creation and purpose and meaning to our lives.

LIVING VALUES

Properly-rooted values become touchstones from which we determine ways of dealing with specific situations. This is not to say that a particular value is always right or should be unchangeable. We need to constantly test our values to ensure their rightness in the context of changing conditions, and our values need to be learned individually through experience, not through intellectual means alone.

"Consider *austerity* as a value, for example. It is something we've thought of as representing unnecessary hardship, meagerness; as something cold and unfriendly. Austerity, however, is a principle which does *not* exclude all enjoyments, only those which are distracting from or destructive of personal relatedness. It is part of a more embracing virtue – friendship or joyfulness – and arises from an awareness that things or tools can destroy rather than enhance grace and joyfulness in personal relations.

Affluence, in contrast, does not discriminate between what is wise and useful and what is merely possible. Affluence demands impossible endless growth, both because those things necessary for good relations are foregone for unnecessary things, and because many of those unnecessary things act to damage or destroy the good relations that we desire."[2]

Austerity, in a garden, eliminates things that distract us from deep connection with a particular cluster of relationships, patterns, and qualities we want to experience.

Deeper and more direct experience brings forth deeper understanding of values and how they clarify and enrich our decisions and our lives. Appendix B lists some value shifts which may have appropriate application as we move deeper into today's new possibilities.

The values we live by must be *living* values – constantly reforged and intensified in our own lives. Under conditions when growth and great material wealth was possible, our values and the actions arising out of them shifted to take best advantage of that possibility. Today conditions have changed. We now see different kinds of benefits holding greater rewards, and our values and actions are again adjusting to harmonize with those new realities.

E.F. Schumacher, in his seminal essay *"Buddhist Economics,"*[3] made clear the vital role of the value base of our economics. In regards to work, he said:

> *"There is a universal agreement that the fundamental source of wealth is human labour. Now, the modern economist has been brought up to consider 'labour' or work as little more than a necessary evil. From the point of view of the employer, it is in any case simply an item of cost, to be reduced to a minimum if it cannot be eliminated altogether, say, by automation. From the point of view of the workman, it is a 'disutility'; to work is to make a sacrifice of one's leisure and comfort, and wages are a kind of compensation for the sacrifice. Hence, the ideal from the point of view of the employer is to have output without employees, and the ideal from the point of view of the employee is to have income without employment.*
>
> *The consequences of these attitudes both in theory and in practice are, of course, extremely far-reaching. If the ideal with regard to work is to get rid of it, every method that 'reduces the work load' is a good thing . . ."*

In contrast, he continues:

> *"The Buddhist point of view takes the function of work to be at least threefold: to give a man a chance to utilize and develop his faculties; to enable him to overcome his ego-centeredness by joining with other people in a common task; and to bring forth the goods and services needed for a becoming existence.*
>
> *Again, the consequences that flow from this view are endless. To organize work in such a manner that it becomes meaningless, boring, stultifying, or nerve-racking for the worker would be little short of criminal, it would indicate a greater concern with goods than with people, an evil lack of compassion and a soul-destroying degree of attachment to the most primitive side of this worldly existence. Equally, to strive for leisure as an*

alternative to work would be considered a complete misunder-standing of one of the basic truths of human existence, namely that work and leisure are complementary parts of the same living process and cannot be separated without destroying the joy of work and the bliss of leisure."

Similarly, J.C Kumarappa sums the matter up as follows:

> *"If the nature of the work is properly appreciated and applied, it will stand in the same relation to the higher faculties as food is to the physical body. It nourishes and enlivens the higher man and urges him to produce the best he is capable of. It directs his freewill along the proper course and disciplines the animal in him into progressive channels. It furnishes an excellent back-ground for man to display his scale of values and develop his personality. . . If a man has no chance of obtaining work he is in a desperate position, not simply because he lacks an income but because he lacks this nourishing and enlivening factor of disci-plined work which nothing can replace."[4]*

Keeping our economics "value-free" has had the result that the economics we have built, the values it embodies, and the kinds of life it makes possible are totally at odds with the deeper values and life-goals we seek. It prevents the very things that generate true health and well-being.

> * An economics of wholeness must be clearly, explicitly, and intractably linked in all its details with values and goals which contribute directly and holistically to personal, cultural, and planetary well-being.

> * Basing our economics on our deepest goals and values is imperative to effectively achieving them.

> * Understanding and linking to our non-material deepest goals, and finding more direct paths to them is utterly essential to achieving the greatest Factor Ten leaps in effec-tiveness of our economic systems.

INTENTION CHANGES LIVES

Our intentions and values can totally change the impacts of all we do.

Out of an intention of making a Head Start Center good for the kids using it, we once asked what would be most wonderful to us as a kid coming in the door. "The smell of good food!" was the unanimous response. This lead us to put the kitchen right in the middle of the building, open to the classrooms and entry. It worked wonderfully, giving parents a place to stop for a cup of coffee and a chat, and to peek around the corner to know their kids were doing okay. It allowed the cook to be an extra friend and source of snacks and hugs for the kids, and a backup pair of eyes for the teachers.

Paying attention to emotional needs of kids, parents, and staff, instead of merely providing "square footage per occupant," and putting this kitchen in the middle of a Head Start Center, opened the door to actions that transformed their lives.

What we didn't realize until later, was how much our intention totally changed working as a cook in this place. Cooking is usually a "back-room" job, tucked away out of sight in service areas near the loading dock. In contrast, putting the cook in the *middle* of everything, and in contact with everyone, made them a central part of what went on. The design which embodied our intention towards the cook's job would change the life of every person who would ever work as a cook in that place.

An architect later asked what we would do if the center was larger and needed a bigger kitchen and loading dock. I looked at him a minute and said, "You've just defined *'too big'*!" Our gut feeling of 'too big' is really connected with a change in intention - from whole-person, meaningful work to mechanical function being dominant.

Valuing the needs of the kids, seeing employees as multi-faceted humans rather than as a job description, and valuing the richness of interaction transformed an institution and the lives of all affected by it.

Aligning our economics and values may seem noble, and there are also significant economic and life-quality benefits in doing so. But the costs of *not* doing so are also demonstrably high. The majority of our intractable social problems today are *diseases of the spirit*, which will be discussed in Chapter Five, resulting from the failure to incorporate life enhancing values in our culture.

These diseases of the spirit are the inevitable and irreducible outcome of an economics which does not have meaningful, nurturing and creative work as a core value and mechanism for attaining our deeper goals. An economics of wholeness which is based on those goals makes them achievable and offers massive savings in the process. It also helps resolve other expensive and intractable existing social problems.

Major changes in economics are necessary in order to achieve the benefits inherent in the essential role that values and non-material goals play in our lives:

* Placing central emphasis in our decision making on what our deepest values and goals are.

* Seeing and evaluating the stream of consequences arising from those goals and actions.

* Including the quantitative and non-quantitative effects of ignoring or displacing goals.

* Reduction in scope of applying *numerical* economics to realms where it is appropriate.

* Testing what we do quantify against the goals sought.

* Reordering economics into a systemic analytical tool to *clarify*, not *quantify*, how alternative courses of action support or impede attainment of our goals.

Non-material and non-quantifiable goals constitute a significant reason for restraint of economics as conventionally practiced. They make clear an order of decision-making that has to take precedence over any traditional economic analysis and also what needs to be infused into any analysis performed.

Limiting the scope and play of numerical economics is simultaneously the assertion of the higher importance of other values and their consequent demand for scope of action. The likely result is the stabilizing of our material culture, but a flowering of ethical and moral growth, artistic achievement, exploration of the vast heights of human potential and the reawakening of social and community life. Its possibilities pale even the greatest achievements of our recent past, and beckon us - not back to the cave - but back to our inner resources and to the incredible potentials of life that they can unfold.

The vastly greater benefits achievable through an economics of wholeness – through its Factor Ten analysis, explicit acknowledgment of non-material goals, limitations of numerical analysis, tools for properly addressing the roles of energy and material resources, the work of ecological systems and life-force energy – provide means for making those changes.

[0] A GUIDE FOR THE PERPLEXED, E. F. Schumacher, 1977.

[1] From *"Izu Principles,"* Tom Bender, Oct. 1994.

[2] See Appendix B, and *"Sharing Smaller Pies,"* Tom Bender, 1974.

[3] *"Buddhist Economics,"* E.F. Schumacher. first published in ASIA: A Handbook, ed. Guy Wint, Anthony Blond Ltd, 1966. Reprinted in ENVIRONMENTAL DESIGN PRIMER, Tom Bender, 1973 and SMALL IS BEAUTIFUL, E.F. Schumacher, 1974, 1999.

[4] ECONOMICS OF PERMANENCE, J.C. Kummarappa, Sarva-Seva Sangh Publications, 1958.

Chapter 4
Ecology and Energy

This chapter is not about "saving the environment." It is about two essential and inescapable elements of successful economics frequently misunderstood and maligned. Ecology and energy have been largely ignored in conventional economics, from lack of understanding, from limitations of economic tools, and also from intent to obscure true costs being shifted onto other parties.

Ecology is vital for several reasons:

* It is the richest available spectrum of on-the-ground, highly-sophisticated, and time-tested "economic" systems, whose patterns can be adapted for our own specific needs.

* Vast amounts of work are done by natural systems, which we benefit from but don't pay for. When we damage those systems, or replace them with industrialized systems, we inherit tremendous costs of doing the work ourselves. "Letting nature do" parts of our systems can dramatically reduce costs.[1]

* Ecological "economic" systems clearly display characteristics – such as optimizing over-systems rather than sub-systems – essential for achieving true efficiencies and effectiveness of economic systems we design.

* Most ecological economic systems are focused on long-term and sustainable operation, based on principles frequently the inverse of our conventional economic systems.

Understanding them can help us develop better working systems of our own:

* Ecological economic systems are based on complexly resilient and cross-benefiting webs of relationships. Conventional economics has attempted a more "engineering" model, of focusing only on single relationships and attempting to optimize them.

* The complex interconnection which actually exists in *all* economic systems results in multiple benefits and costs of any proposed action. Ecology can help us learn to incorporate this kind of interconnection and multiple effects in what we do.

* Apparently similar alternatives being examined may have major differences in dimensions we are not examining. (See Endgame Analysis, below)

Energy (and material) resources are also vital, and their role in tremendous flux at present:

* Energy and material resource perspectives help distinguish between use of capital and income resources, which are very different. Employing *capital* resources (such as fossil fuels) is using up an irreplaceable stock of wealth. On the other hand, *not* employing *income* resources, like solar energy, is forever losing that potential wealth.

* The twentieth-century economy was based on intensive use of non-renewable energy sources to multiply the work we could accomplish. The work needed to recover reserves of fossil fuels was, on the average, only about two percent of the work which those resources could accomplish for us. In effect, we each had five energy-slaves working for us. Competing against such cheap work with our own direct labor, or that of others, was suicidal. Today's new Factor Ten improvements in resource productivity complexifies the picture even further. How increasing productivity of energy *use* plays out against decreasing productivity of *obtaining* the energy resources vs. *shifts* to renewables is yet unclear. Careful attention to what energy resources contribute to our economics is required as the picture evolves.

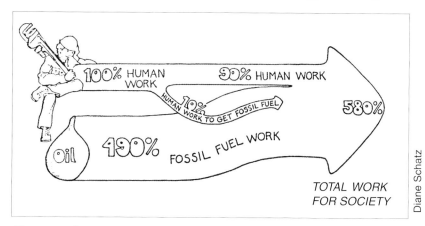

The ease of obtaining the work of fossil fuels has given each of us the equivalent of many energy slaves that it is suicide to compete against with our own work.

* Our economic systems have become dependent upon massive use of fossil fuels, which are being rapidly depleted and whose irreplaceability and increasing costs are not factored into conventional accounting. How this depletion will play out against implementation of resource efficient processes is another uncertainty which needs monitoring.

* The wealth of twentieth-century economics largely represented an outrageous appropriation of irreplaceable natural resources – from soils to groundwater to fossil fuels to concentrated metal ores, rather than any inherent rightness in its goals. Today's wealth needs to come from wise use, rather than magnitude of use.

* International monetary policies have resulted in a desperate competition between indebted countries to export raw materials, causing a flooding of materials markets and prices which fail to reflect long-term impacts of depletion and overuse.

* Our use patterns end up dispersing irreplaceable material resources. Costs of disposal and/or recollection have been ignored.

* The concept of *net energy* has important implications as we make a transition away from intense use of energy resources. Many industrial processes and alternative energy sources

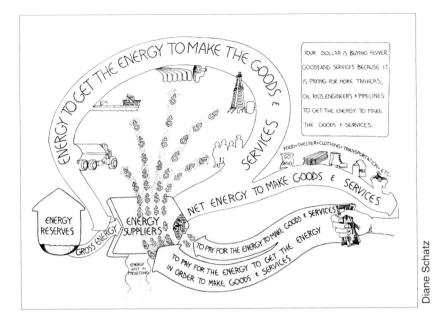

NET ENERGY – The proportion of each unit of energy we produce that is used up to obtain the next unit increases as we use up the cheapest and most readily available resources. Many "apparent" energy sources do not produce net energy once we subtract the energy needed to obtain them.

depend on today's plentiful and cheap energy use for their production. Often they consume more energy in the process than they can potentially provide through their own use. Much of today's agriculture consumes more energy than it produces. Low-grade ores and shale oil require massive energy inputs that will make them unaffordable as energy prices escalate.[2]

* The issue of energy *quality* is generally ignored in both engineering and economic considerations. Waste heat from a high-temperature application can be used in a low-temperature application, getting double productivity out of the resource. Some sources are "cleaner" than others; some, such as electricity, are capable of uses others can't accomplish; and some, such as petroleum products, are more concentrated and easily portable than others such as wood.

* Factor Ten improvements in energy/resource productivity and institutional performance are in the process of fundamentally transforming all of our systems of production and distribution of material goods and services.

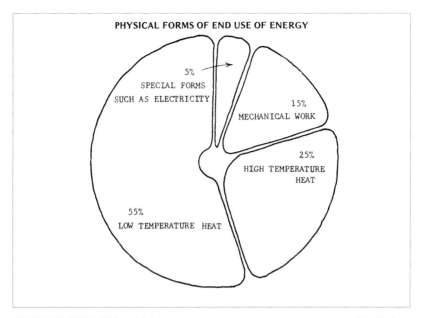

ENERGY QUALITY – *A high temperature energy source can provide high temperature heat, such as for steel-making, and the lower-temperature waste heat from that can be used for lower-temperature applications, such as heating of buildings.*

ECOLOGICAL CONNECTEDNESS

The most important aspect of ecology concerning economics is not the familiar "environmental" concern about pollution. It is the simple and familiar adage, *"All things are connected."* We are used to looking at economics from an "engineering" perspective excluding as many of the less vital connections as possible, and focussing only on issues and actions central to achieving the results we seek.

But everything is connected by a complex web of relationships. Secondary effects outside of how we are used to looking at something may ultimately be more vital and have greater economic impact. And even if they are of lesser magnitude than our primary concerns, when added together, their *cumulative sum* is frequently far greater than our primary concern.

> *When we use an ecologically-based rather than engineering-based perspective in economics, we end up with a new arithmetic. When we see the whole web of costs and benefits, we see that they add up to more than the 100% in an engineered system.*

* *In ecological arithmetic, 1+1=3.*

* *It always takes more than one solution to solve a problem.*

* *Any real solution solves more than one problem.*

Let's look at water-flushed toilets, for example. They may be a simple and sanitary way of getting sewage out of our houses. Using a pipe to dump the sewage in a river may be the cheapest way of getting rid of it. But when we consider the next community downstream, and add in the cost of their having to repurify the drinking water we've just dumped our sewage into, we have a secondary impact that may be greater than the primary cost of our sewers.

Looking upstream, we have a secondary cost of having had to repurify the drinking water we use to flush our toilets, because the community upstream dumped their sewage into it. In the stream itself, we can see other health costs, fishery losses, etc. And looking at the farms along the river, we can see the cost of having to apply expensive fertilizers to replace the nutrients which left the fields in our foods, and which we flushed down the river instead of returning to the fields.

Without even considering fundamentally different alternative systems of handling our sewage, many communities have already found that *giving away* new low-flush or waterless toilets to reduce water demand is far cheaper than developing new water supplies, plus water costs, plus expanded sewage treatment systems, plus the cost of treating the sewage. All those systems are connected, and we ultimately pay all the costs. A change in one part affects all of them, and we need to track the connections, costs, and benefits throughout the entire web affected. When we don't, new and expensive problems pop up elsewhere that we have to deal with.

Looking at heating efficiency of buildings can show us that a whole range of tools can give different perspectives on obtaining higher performance, and that some solutions work together, while others cancel or eliminate opportunity for another. When I was in architecture school, we were told that oil or gas heat only converted about half the energy in the fuel into usable heat, and that electric resistance heating was 100% efficient. All the energy in the wires was converted to heat in the building. (This boiled down really to an issue of on-site capital and space costs.) Then we learned about heat pumps (air conditioners are heat pumps), which needed less energy to *pump* heat into or out of a space than to heat or cool a space directly. (A higher quality form of energy was able to use a different technique to achieve a goal.)

Much later, after I got out of school, we learned to trace the electric wires back to where they came from. (Cradle to grave costs, losses in converting one form of energy to another, transmission losses.) We found, of course, that the conversion of fuels into electricity was even more wasteful compared to efficient use of the fuel to heat the building directly or using waste heat from the electrical generation to heat the building. (Cascading energy uses, finding application from lower quality waste heat) And even later, we realized that using the energy to make insulation to insulate the building *so we didn't have to heat it* was even *more* efficient. (Avoiding problems)

The yardsticks we use to evaluate how well we're doing change dramatically when we use different boundaries around what we are looking at. *Understanding the web of connections inherent in all ecological systems helps us begin to find boundaries which dramatically reduce overall costs.*

ECOLOGICAL SOPHISTICATION

Processes used in natural systems are often far more sophisticated, resource conserving and effective that our present industrial systems. Simple biological systems produce complex chemicals in minute and precise scale without the immense temperatures, pressures, and complex processes we have employed in industry. Mollusks drill holes through hard rock without destroying their shells through use of enzymes that dissolve the rock. There is evidence that ancient builders in MezoAmerica and Cambodia used plant-sourced "epoxies" to glue their rock structures together rather than using mortar that would dissolve over time in the humid tropic rainforests. The endocrine systems in our bodies produce and regulate extremely complex and effective drugs.[3]

Attempts are underway, both with nano-technology to produce molecular-scaled computers and tools and with biologic-based chemical and pharmaceutical production to adapt the wisdom and sophistication of ecological systems to our own needs. These will provide further order-of-magnitude improvements in energy and material productivity.

END-GAME ANALYSIS[4]

Endgame thinking involves figuring out what kind of a position we want to be in down the road, when actions we are committing ourselves to today have made their effect. It helps us choose alternative actions according to what situation they will leave us with in addition to their initial, or even their lifecycle costs.

Alternate courses of action with apparently equivalent financial, environmental, and social costs may also actually leave us in *entirely* different end positions. Both the processes involved and the "ecological connectedness" of alternatives can be fundamentally different. This is particularly true when dealing with resource-based processes, finite material and energy resources and/or systems with differing elements of eternal (long-lived) vs. ephemeral (consumable) goods.

Let's look first at using fossil fuels vs. passive solar energy to heat a building. Assume that the cost of both over a twenty year period is the same, and both have similar environmental effects.

At the end of the twenty years, however, the fossil fuel alternative ends with an empty fuel tank and a furnace needing replacement. In contrast, the solar energy alternative leaves us with a heating system in place ready to continue heating the building for several hundred more years. In addition, we still have the original fossil fuel reserves for our future benefit, likely to be worth more in addition. The residual value (fuel reserves) is significant. The prospect (continuing free solar heating) is equally significant. Both need to be included in a true comparison of alternatives.

One alternative consumed capital resources, the other was supported by a continuing income. Said differently, *solar energy not used today is gone tomorrow, while fuels not used are worth more tomorrow!* When we fail to make such distinctions in our analyses as either individuals or a society as a whole, we can easily end up in unnecessary and uncomfortable situations.

Should a nation support global sourcing for components in everything from cars to computers? This may permit some financial savings. It may also, however, destroy our independent manufacturing capability to support a major war in the future, which could be disastrous from a national security perspective. But then again, such interdependence might avoid that war.

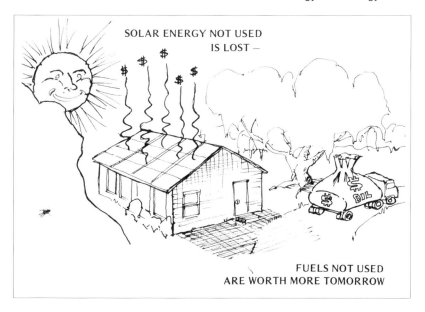

Other cultures, our economic competitors today, are used to thinking in terms of hundred and thousand year time increments and strategies which ensure their best endgame situation over such time periods. It is time we began to do so as well.

Endgame positions can also be strongly affected by the *sequence* in which choices are made. Compare two households, each anticipating purchasing several expensive vacations plus a house over the next ten years. The household which purchases the vacations before the house ends up with memories, and a house. The household which purchases the house *before* the vacations ends up with memories, a house, plus perhaps $50-$60,000 in home equity!

> ENDGAME: *Expenditures on durables before consumables reap enduring benefits.*

> Take this comparison one step further. Family A bought their house before vacations, but bought a house with an expected use life of 40 years. Family B does the same, but spends 20% more for a house which will last 400 years. Forty years later they both retire and sell their houses. Family A gets out just before the roof falls in. Family B gets 90% of their entire investment back.

ENDGAME: *Durability pays. And pays. And pays.*

And what happens with Family C, who built a durable house, paid cash, and built for energy efficiency? They set up an additional stream of events which could result in a 75% savings on housing expenditures for themselves and their descendents![5]

Endgame thinking really shines looking at *series* of actions:

Something of value in a single situation may become a disaster when repeated.

Let's look at automobile purchase, for example. We're told that time-payment or credit buying, has benefits that justify the cost. We are able to have use of what we're buying while we pay for it instead of having to wait until we've saved the money for its purchase. Some truth there – maybe – in a single occurrence. But let's look down the road a bit, at the end of that game, or better yet a few games later.

After forty to fifty years, we've bought and financed ten cars, let's say, and given ourselves the same rationale each time. Let's compare that option to a "cash" scenario, where we'd gone without, or driven a junker, or used transit, or shared a vehicle while we saved to buy *just the first car.*

After the *first* purchase, we're not going without a vehicle in *either* scenario. The debt-financing option ends up with possible use benefit during the *first* vehicle's life, but with interest payments on *ten* vehicles. Pay-as-you-go ends up with possible partial inconvenience during the first vehicle's life, and *no* inconvenience or interest payments during the ownership of the other nine vehicles. In the first case, the endgame is the cost of fifty years of interest payments. In the second case, we end with fifty years of interest *income* on savings to accumulate the principal to purchase each subsequent vehicle.

This distinction applies just as much to single vs. continuing use of credit-card purchasing, compared to keeping our expenditures within our flows of income revenue or saving to make a series of purchases.

ENDGAME: *We only benefit from debt financing the first time we use it.*

On subsequent purchases financing is a major expense with no concomitant benefit. Additionally, that first debt purchase frequently pushes us into a cycle of continuing debt purchasing, where we're trapped with no real benefit. Interest and principal payments on the original debt prevent us from saving for subsequent purchases. (See Chapter Eight)

We can also see that if we adopt a pay-as-you-go pattern generally, the savings generated quickly allow us to immediately pay cash for purchases rather than having to wait until we've saved up the cost. This overrides even the original justification and value of debt financing.

These alternatives represent <u>MAJOR</u> differences in cumulative costs. When we apply endgame thinking to our personal expenditure patterns as a whole, including car and home payments, credit card purchases, etc. we see we're talking a cost difference amounting to maybe *ten years of net income,* and even more pretax income! A pretty heavy price for sloppy shopping.

In the public realm, debt-financing (such as bonded capital improvement) results in our paying DOUBLE what those improvements would otherwise cost. Debt financing in the public realm is one of perhaps a half-dozen baseline reasons our public expenditures have become unaffordable.

A city needs a new $10 million sewage treatment plant and votes in a 30 year bond issue to pay for it. No one mentions that the actual total cost to pay off the bonds is probably $20 million, not $10 million. A few years later the city needs a new school; later, a new hospital; later still, street improvements; and then a new landfill or water treatment plant. Because of the finance charges from earlier debts, it can't revenue-finance the subsequent ones, and has to bond-finance them as well.

The reality is that capital investments are a consistent ongoing process of every city, county, state or national government. The government that plans ahead sees roughly what improvements will be needed, and when. Then they get those needs queued up so that each can be financed in turn out of current revenues. An unanticipated investment can be financed through a one-time levy. Improvements are obtained at half the cost and with freedom of action that the debt-financing entity has lost.

Similarly, higher education systems can maintain an ongoing budget item for construction. Campus A may get a new physics building this year, then campus B gets a new gym next year, and Campus C gets some new dormitories two or three years later, all financed out of current revenues.

Proponents of public debt-financing point to low interest costs, and talk about inflation resulting in "lower cost of repayment dollars." Interest rates on loans, however, already include a projection for anticipated inflation in addition to true interest rates sought by the lender. The length of most public capital improvement bonds is also long enough that interest represents a higher proportion of repayment costs than on personal loans, and means that more "old loans" are having to be paid for each year instead of paying cash for current expenditures.

Looked at in aggregate, by examining the financial records of almost any public body over a forty or fifty year period, we see:

* Consistent patterns and levels of continuing capital expenditures, virtually all debt-financed after the first occurrence of debt-financing.

* Repayment demands each year of twenty to thirty years of old debts, not just current ones.

* Total debt service on old debts each year running about as high as current expenditures (excluding their commitments to future debt repayment costs).

Aggregate patterns of expenditures, and real world records demonstrate clearly that revenue-financing instead of debt-financing would consistently have achieved the same series of improvements for half the cost.

Endgame thinking reveals how carefully we sometimes avoid looking at the overall costs of our actions. Ask yourself what you paid for your house or car. Did you include the total financing cost in your answer? Few people do. Do you even *know,* in dollars, how much the *total* financing is going to cost you?

Next time you vote, take a look at bond issue explanations on the ballot. Odds are that they give just the *net* amount sought from the bond issue, instead of telling you the *total* amount we are going to have to pay to provide the net proceeds, *plus* financing costs, *plus* tax avoidance makeup for tax-free bonds.

You can make another check on your financial reality avoidance if you have recently sold a house or some property. Ask yourself if you made a profit on the sale. Then check if you made that conclusion by just comparing the purchase and resale price. Examine what difference there is when you deduct realtor's commissions, taxes, and financing charges you paid while you owned it, and currency inflation. Compare the result to what you would have made in interest if you had put the money in the bank or invested it elsewhere.

At its very least, endgame strategy offers opportunity for major financial resource redirection – from illusory benefits of debt financing into expenditures which can give lasting benefit to society.

FORESTRY ECONOMICS

A look at forestry economics can show the role that ecological visioning can give to economic systems, how a Factor Ten economics case study can develop from gut feelings to hard numbers, and the connection between the work that nature does and the effectiveness of our industrial systems.[6]

Forestry, like many social issues, has become caught in a gridlock between those who wish to preserve a resource and those who want to maximize the immediate benefits from it. This particular study came about from two causes:

* A feeling that adversarial issues arise out of lack of broad enough perspective to accommodate and interrelate divergent viewpoints, and that seeking a win/win solutions might provide better benefits to *all* parties.

* A gut feeling that our forestry practices are neither ecologically wise nor economically competent. Little did I suspect the *magnitude* of the benefits that would become apparent.

Living in the Maritime Pacific Northwest, in an area where 85% of the land is in commercial timber production, visceral evidence of our forestry practices is inescapable. In my gut, they felt very wrong. At first I thought this was a reaction to clear-cuts and stump fields, but I'd worked on farms and been in forests where logging was carried out in ways which didn't give me a wrench in the gut. It wasn't an issue of preserving pristine ancient forests, as wonderful as they are. Something also kept nagging at me about sunlight – about acres of stumps and foot-high tree seedlings not capturing all the sunlight, which runs the whole show.

This is the first step in a successful Factor Ten analysis: a practice you know is based on short-term thinking which hasn't been looked at systematically, and an intuitive hunch where the roots of a solution might be.

I'd been given a collection of research papers by a local forestry group, which contained two nuggets – an economic study of coastal forests by an independent forester, Mark Wigg, which showed that long-rotation forestry could be economically more productive,[7] and a group of government forestry studies which showed both net economic loss from many conventional forestry practices, and the economic value of non-timber-production uses of forests. Putting the two together gave both incredulous figures of the economic value of long-rotation timber production, and an understanding of the underlying shortcomings and blind spots of our conventional forestry economics that had kept us from seeing the whole picture.

Here are the conclusions I pulled together:

LONG ROTATIONS can <u>double</u> sustainable yields of timber, while providing an amazing <u>nine-fold</u> increase in net economic returns from timber production.

* CLEARCUTS *are reduced by 75%* in going from 60 to 240 year rotations, resulting in significantly more land in real forests with multiple-use possibilities.

FISHERIES restoration possible with long rotation harvesting *can produce annual revenues in the order of seven to twenty times current timber revenues.*

RECREATION development possible with long rotation harvesting *can produce annual revenues in the order of five to ten times current timber revenues.*

SPECIAL FOREST PRODUCTS harvest, such as mushrooms and medicinals, possible with long rotation harvesting, *can produce significant annual revenues.*

* TOTAL net economic value of long rotation forest management thus appears to be roughly <u>twenty</u> to <u>thirty</u> times that of present management practices.

These new Factor Ten numbers might well seem hard to believe. But once we see the actual elements involved and the reasons for the magnitude of cost differences it becomes quite clear that conventional forestry economics has been missing some rather significant elements. Here are some of the vital elements that have been ignored:

* Every cut cycle loses about 15 years of solar energy fueled wood production – growth time lost through cutting and replanting, time to reestablish root and photosynthetic area and for seedlings to grow to capture total sunlight falling on an area. The first 15 years of growth is represented by the unmerchantable top of the tree which is cut off at harvest, and the other seedlings that are eventually shaded out by the more mature trees.

* Timber production does not drop off significantly beyond the traditional harvest (CMAI) point for many, many years. Harvest cycles can be extended several times the conventional 60 year rotations while still staying quite near the maximum productivity. Such practices also typically produce a higher percentage of high value wood in larger logs. Long rotation harvests produce almost twice as many board feet and 25% more cubic feet than short rotation.

* Timber management costs have huge impact on net economic yield. Cutting, replanting, and thinning – expensive and dangerous work – occur during the early growth part of the cycle. Longer rotations which minimize these repeated management costs require less work and expense, and produce far greater net economic returns. We should pay those people to do other, *productive*, work for society – not work that results in *less* timber yield.

* The <u>non-timber</u> product value of forest lands far exceeds that of timber production, and has been ignored and damaged by past forestry practices:

> – Forest Service studies in 1989 and 1990 showed tourism, hunting, and recreation producing $122

billion vs. logging revenues of $13 billion – ten times as great.

– A 1990 Forest Service study showed that recreation fees could be three times as great as revenues from timber.

– Salmon from the Smith River in California, even heavily damaged by logging, produced $7.8 million/year – more than the entire logging revenues from the basin.

– A Forest Service study on the Salmon River in Idaho showed that a $14 million logging operation resulted in a $100 million salmon revenue loss.

* *Inappropriate accounting practices have ignored these major costs and benefits in favor of immediate financial gains through quicker logging.* Impacts of practices in one area (timber production) on the productivity of other areas (fisheries and recreation, for example) were ignored. Present Net Value accounting, most widely used, places small increases in immediate revenues ahead of the cost of major revenue loss in later years. By starting conceptually with a bare acre of land, it assumes interest rates on "investments" made to plant, thin, and manage, which are not investments but required restoration costs of *harvest*. It also assumes replanting costs to be unavoidable, while we see that with longer rotations, several cycles of those major costs *are* avoidable. In maximizing immediate rather than total financial return, PNV almost invariably causes timber to be cut before it reaches its maximum cumulative average growth.

* *Taxpayer subsidy of federal forestry programs result in artificially low timber prices* and major revenue losses to *private* timberland owners. Over $5.6 billion of taxpayer dollars was lost by the U.S. Forest Service in one decade from subsidizing of logging sales. The impact on reducing market value of competing private timber would be many times as great.

* *Long-rotation timber harvest can sustain timber yields that would otherwise be lost* from the disease, nutrient loss, soil losses, and fungal destruction of current timber management practices. Northwest Oregon coastal forests have exceed-

ingly high risk of erosion causing soils loss impacting both timber and fisheries. Long rotations dramatically lessen soils disturbance and loss affecting fisheries and timber production and their revenues. Soil microorganism health issues also play a much more vital role than previously suspected in the reforestation success, productivity, and disease-resistance of forest stands.

These omissions include lack of understanding the ecological basis of the systems involved, lack of an inclusive systematic view of benefits from the forests, and use of accounting tools intended to skew decision-making. Proper assessment of management alternatives requires examination of *all* revenue sources, associated *costs* as well as income, and the interaction and effects of management practices of one area on the productivity of other areas. With such assessment, the true value of alternatives such as long rotation forestry become quite clear, as well as the need for understanding the ecological and energetic basis of the systems involved.

Let's look at the results of quadrupling timber harvest rotations in terms of the categories of savings discussed in Chapter Two:

Resource productivity in timber is doubled (2X) by eliminating 75% of the "fallow time" caused by each cut cycle. In the real world, resource productivity is increased by probably another 2X because the genetically-altered, "fast-growing" trees currently growing on commercial timberland have turned out (as many warned) to be highly disease-susceptible, producing only half of expected growth. Productivity is increased further in that higher quality timber is produced (fewer knots, tighter grain, higher structural strength), giving a total timber productivity increase of 4-5X. Human work productivity increases 4X by eliminating three out of four cuts. Equipment and fuel productivity is increased by probably 3-4X. Fisheries productivity is increased 7X. Special forest products such as mushrooms and medicinal herbs increase by probably a similar amount.

Institutional/financial productivity gains include 9X (or 18X) gains in net financial returns on timber production, 7X fisheries financial gain, 5X-10X recreational value gains, for a total financial productivity gain of 20-35X.

Goal effectiveness gains include biodiversity benefits of more mature forests, clearcutting reduced by 75%, forest area needed for equivalent timber production reduced by 4-5X. 20-30X financial gains are available for other benefits to society. 75% of dangerous human work involved is eliminated, allowing (with the 20-30X financial benefits released) those people to be employed in more socially productive projects – building schools or improving healthcare.

Connected systems impacts include the fisheries gain, forest products gains, forest and aquatic health improvements; reduction in landslides and soils loss; safer and more socially-beneficial employment; greater carbon sequestering.

So an economics of wholeness that tracks, seeks, and attains such major improvements in different dimensions of economic value can produce diverse and highly significant benefit to our lives. Properly approached, it can be a win-win situation for everyone.

---

[1] See TOWARD A STEADY-STATE ECONOMY, ed. Herman E. Daly, W.H. Freeman, 1973; STEADY-STATE ECONOMICS, Herman E. Daly, W.H. Freeman, 1977; VALUING THE EARTH: Economics, Ecology, Ethics, ed. Herman E. Daly and Kenneth N. Townsend, M.I.T. Press, 1993; and ECOLOGICAL AND GENERAL SYSTEMS, H.T. Odum, Univ. Press of Colorado, 1994.

[2] See ENVIRONMENT, POWER, AND SOCIETY, Howard T. Odum, Wiley-Interscience, 1970; ENERGY BASIS FOR MAN AND NATURE, H.T. and Elisabeth C. Odum, McGraw-Hill, 1976.

[3] See BIOMIMICRY, Janine Benyas, Wm. Morrow & Co., 1997.

[4] *"Endgame Analysis,"* Tom Bender, Nov. 1990, IN CONTEXT, July 1996.

[5] See *"The Hidden Cost of Housing,"* Tom Bender. RAIN MAGAZINE, Mar/ Apr 1984. Reprinted in UTNE READER, Summer 1984; SUN TIMES, Nov/ Dec 1984; ALTERNATIVE PRESS ANNUAL, 1984.

[6] *"Improving the Economic Value of Coastal Public Forest Lands,"* Tom Bender, Dec. 1994, IN CONTEXT, July 1996.

[7] *"The Economics of Sustainable Forestry,"* Mark Wigg. SOCIETY OF AMERICAN FORESTERS, 1989.

Chapter 5
Life-Force Energy and the Sacred

It is a rare time when profound change in the direction of society occurs. Sometimes it occurs quietly, out of public view, and is slow to leave visible trace on society. A shift in political balance in the Christian church occurred in the Council of Nicaea in AD 325, for example, which excommunicated clergy who taught direct experience of the sacred, transforming the church – and European society – into one which acknowledged only the material world, with some hope for "salvation" after death.

In AD 869 at the Council of Constantinople, the church banned the concept of reincarnation. Out of their direct experience of the sacred, people like John Scotus Erigena were stating that our spiritual selves are eternal, do not completely embody themselves in an incarnation, but go through many incarnations for further development. Again the church politicians chose to deny this broadly accepted awareness, though it lived on in the mystery schools at Chartres and elsewhere which gave birth to the spiritual passion of Gothic Europe.[1] Out of this repeated censure of spiritual experience came the European Renaissance and our current culture.

At other times, major changes occur dramatically, bringing rapid and visible transformation in the culture. The mastery of the use of fossil fuels and the atom bomb in the 19th and 20th century brought swift and dramatic transformation to global society.

One of these profound shifts is in process in our culture today – a deeper understanding of the spiritual dimension of our existence, and with it reacknowledgment of the existence of life-force energy. This shift is likely to bring transformative changes surpassing even that achieved by all of our physical sciences over the last two centuries.

Called *chi* in Chinese, *prana* in Hindu, *baraka* in Arabic, *ka* or *ankh* in Egyptian, *itz* or *ch'ulel* in Maya traditions, life-force energy has been central to the cosmology, healing arts, sciences and arts of virtually every culture in history other than our own. It underlies acupuncture, the chakra system in our bodies, our informational connection with other life; Maya, Egyptian, Chinese, Islamic and Gothic sacred architecture; fire-walking, dowsing, remote viewing, hands-on healing, and what we have called "psychic phenomena" of many kinds. The CIA uses it for "remote viewing." Police use it to find missing people. Many people have precognitive dreams or premonitions.

Current research in many of the sciences is indicating that life-force energy and intention form the templates upon which all material objects manifest from the world of spirit.

Egyptian goddess transmitting healing energy to a Pharaoh.

Not only ourselves, but all life, and all things in our surroundings are manifested, nurtured, healed, and communicate through the vehicle of chi energy. It is responsible for vitality, for our energetic survival after death, and for personal, community and cultural health throughout the world.

It is only recently that we have had research equipment sensitive enough to confirm the existence of the acupuncture meridians in our bodies, EEG and other bodily changes occurring during hands-on healing, and the replicability of other related phenomena. Life-force energy does not fit into the existing conceptual framework of our physical sciences and the beliefs of how our universe operates which have evolved out of that framework. Like past major advances in our sciences, it is bringing an expansion and reformulation of that framework, with Nobel Prize-winning research in physics currently bringing related quantum theory closer to experienced reality each year. As our understanding matures, it brings fundamental revision in our concepts of life, death, health, evolution, philosophy and the goals towards which we apply our economic systems.[2]

What does something so seemingly esoteric as chi energy have to do with economics? Like harnessing fossil fuels or splitting the atom, it brings a major change in the focus of our society, and in turn economics. Fossil fuels brought the age of industry and a wonderful deepening of our ability to manifest things on the material level. The atomic age again altered our dreams, towards exploring the heavens, and towards unfettering our imaginations as to what we and our world could become.

Chi energy touches the deepest roots of our concepts of our world, of life and death, of the meaning of existence. It is in process of

The Kiyomizu Shrine in Kyoto is built on a massive wood substructure to center it on a strong energy point on the ridge of the hill.

transforming our sciences as well. It is bringing to bear the same powerful focus of attention we've lavished on the material world, now onto the world of spirit. It is transforming our goals – now onto the inner product of work to the degree we've focused on the outer product, and on the growth of inner qualities to balance what we've achieved in outer ones. Both what we seek and how we seek it changes.

Like the realm of values we discussed in Chapter Three, chi brings into the balance things which are vital, yet which are unquantifiable. Limitations of the tools we've employed in economics become clearly apparent, and in truth, valuing of "efficiency" in decision-making becomes far less central.

Additionally, as the import of chi energy works its way through our health, education, work, governing, justice and other dimensions of society, the means we employ to achieve conventional goals is changing. When we become aware how little of something we've just discovered came from our own minds and how much was channeled through from the spirit world, our processes of education and research change. When we realize how much the success of a project we've been hard at work on was dependent on alignment of energies in the cosmos, assistance from our ancestors, or co-creation with other life, we begin to pay attention to different means of project management. When we see how our homes, workplaces and communities change as chi energy becomes a root element of design and building, what we program into our buildings, services, and products is transformed.[3]

Without an understanding of life-force energetics, we've attempted to heal emotional, spiritual and psychological damages from abuse, rape, homelessness and other manifestations of diseases of the spirit through expensive and marginally effective techniques such as psychiatry and counseling. New energy-based techniques working directly with the bodily-embedded energetic effects of such damage and with group ritual are achieving remarkably rapid, effective, and affordable success which has not been possible through conventional healing techniques.[4]

Here are some of the changes we can expect as the reacknowledgment of chi energy progresses:

* Revolutionizing of processes and techniques employed in medicine and healing, transportation, education and other sectors of our economy.

Combining resource productivity, institutional effectiveness, life-force energy and the sacred can lead to buildings, such as this community bank on the Oregon coast, that place fewer demands on our ecological systems and generate more positive effects on their community and the people who work in them.

* Fundamental transformation of our understanding of our universe; expansion of the framework of our physical sciences, and transmuting of their technological applications.

* Reconnection with the rest of Creation, realization of our oneness with other life, co-creation, co-evolution; a vital sense of Oneness with other people, other life, and with the purpose and ongoing dance of Creation.

* Expansion of the frontiers of our imagination, dreams, desires, and aspirations.

* Expanding our cultural focus from the material world to embrace as well other dimensions of our existence.

* Transformation of our personal and institutional relation-ships and individual missions in life. A sense of "for-the-good-of all" pervading our existence and actions.

* Development of new goals for society and our lives. A major increase in the qualitative rather than the quantitative, and in transcendent rather than material aspects of our lives.

* Alteration of business goals, desire for material goods, work patterns, the value and psychological base of economic activity.

* A basic change in our perspectives towards the nature of death, its role in life, and of our lives transcending it.

* A reconnection with the spirit world; the wisdom, perspec-tive, support and assistance it can give us. Understanding of spirit's active role in our lives, through the medium of chi energy.

* Access to vastly deeper and more powerful processes of learning.

* Transformation of our ethics and values.

Through a process called *quantum entanglement*, discovered op-erating even on the level of sub-atomic particles, any changes, any-where in our universe, are communicated instantly to everything ever in contact with what was affected.[5] Communicated *instantly, unlimited by the speed of light*. We are seamlessly informed and inform – on a sub-atomic, cellular, organismic, and community level. Our inner beings know and speak the truth of our existence and know and speak the truth of all we've ever touched or been touched by. *We cannot lie.*

Once we understand that, and begin again to listen to our inner voices, we can hear every nuance in the flood of deceit which is poured upon us daily. We can hear it, and we can hear what *is* true. With that, we have entered a new world.

A world where we no longer can lie, where our innermost thoughts are accessible to all, is a world of transformed business practices and goals. Work which nurtures and develops skills; industry whose goal is effortlessly and imperturbably meeting *needs*, not creating *desires*; mechanisms of exchange which are based on giving, sharing, and honesty rather than deceit become the template upon which successful commerce is built.

An economics of wholeness needs an integrative understanding of underlying energetic mechanisms of our universe which chi energy provides, because that, we are discovering, is how our universe *does* work. The reemergence of chi energy, with new clarity and stripped of encrustations of time and accumulated error, gives us awareness of how spirit and values are coming to impact our lives and the tools we use to clarify and assist our decisions. It is essential to attaining the full potentials of Factor Ten economics both in the clarifying of our goals and in providing more direct and effortless mechanisms to achieve those goals.

THE SACRED
Uniquely connected with life-force energy in having a pivotal new impact on economics is a transformed understanding of the sacred coming into focus today. What is emerging is not the once-a-week attendance-at-church which satisfied the diminished role of spirit in a culture focused on the material. Instead, we are discovering that sacredness has to do with, and transforms, every aspect of our everyday world. It underlies, but is distinct from, the religious expressions of the sacred which often tend to separate us from others with different spiritual traditions. It is a vital element to focus and direct our own energies and marshal other energies to help in our accomplishing our goals.[6]

We need the sacred as part of our economics because:

* Rooting our lives in the sacred is the only way to ensure working, living, and social patterns that enable and nurture healthy lives that avoid our currently endemic diseases of the spirit.

* It is cheaper to revere all life and hold it safe than to incur the costs of patchwork environmental laws, regulations, litigation and enforcement – or the cost of their absence.

* Economics based on the sacred directs our actions more positively, directly, and effectively toward our individual and social goals.

* Its absence is the root cause of modern religious fundamentalism and terrorism and their associated costs.

* Its nurture is a great reward in itself – attainable in no other way.

HOLDING THINGS SACRED

Whenever we allow ourselves to know a place, person, or thing intimately, we come to love them. We see among their inevitable warts and wrinkles the special and wonderful things that they are, and their existence becomes as precious to us as our own. Loving them, we come to hold their existence inviolate – or sacred – and any action which would harm them becomes inconceivable. Openness, intimacy, knowledge, and love are the essential foundations upon which any healthy existence is built.

We know in our own lives that if a person/place/world we love is not happy, we can't be happy. *We soon discover that our well-being is dependent in large part on our contribution to the well-being of others* and of all life. As we reach out and come to know our world more intimately, we come to love each piece of it, and hold it sacred. This leads, inevitably, to discovering the sacredness of *all* places, *all* things, and *all* life; approaching all life in a sacred manner; and inhabiting, therefore, a sacred world. As part of a sacred world, we ourselves – individually and collectively – are to be held sacred also. And that calls forth a totally different way of relating and acting.

In a world that cherishes and holds sacred *all* life, there is no room for taking for greed rather than for need. In it we rediscover the multiple benefits of giving and sharing, and the healing nurture of relationships based on love and the sacred. This implements fundamental change in our ways of working, playing, celebrating, sharing, and shaping our surroundings. We find a new strength and vitality arising in all parts of our lives. Much of this framework lies outside of what has traditionally been considered economics. But any powerful force in the efficacy of materializing our dreams is something that must be part of any economics of wholeness.

The sacred — in our lives, our actions, our surroundings, and the processes by which we interact — is essential for our well-being. We cannot have strong and clear intention that leads to real success in our lives unless all parts of our lives have coherence and resonate with the same core values. Even our surroundings concretely reflect the values which were inherent in their making, and it is essential that we bring both our places and our values into coherence as they reflect back into our lives.

And finally, we have a need for the sacred in our economics because it is inherent in how our universe operates. Evolution (and life) requires a dynamic balance and tension between harmony, balance, and stasis on one hand, and emergence of new and possibly destructive possibilities on the other. Love, giving, and holding sacred are the glue which maintains and holds together this churning, chaotic dance. If we deny the existence and role of vital aspects of our universe in how we live and do things which affect the world around us, we ask for and create only problems.

DISEASES OF THE SPIRIT

We ignore the sacred today in part because we fail to see the commonness in the many symptoms of illness that arise from its absence in our lives. We ignore it also because we fail to understand the mechanisms by which the sacred affects and nurtures our lives and our health. We see ourselves surrounded by apparently intractable social problems — violence, alcoholism, drug use, crime, child abuse, apathy, failing schools, obesity. All are reaching epidemic proportions. All seem resistant to resolving.

These are not, however, separate problems. They are all symptoms of disease — not in our bodies, but in our psychic "immune systems" that keep always-present situations from escalating into epidemic problems. These social problems all arise out of the same lack of self-worth, lack of respect by and for others, or lack of opportunity to be of use and value to family and society. These problems are all a single *disease of the spirit.*

This *disease of the spirit* is the same one we see in the eyes of people who have been defeated – individually or as a society – and who have seen what they love and value destroyed, lost, or taken away. It is the same disease of the spirit when wealth and comfort make us too self-satisfied to reach out for the vital nourishment and understanding arising from work, community, and giving to others. It is the same disease of the spirit where we lack the nurture of meaningful and honored goals, roles, responsibilities and power.

The numbers of dysfunctional people in our schools and cities is increasing rapidly – people damaged by lack of love, not being valued, absence of opportunity; by resultant abuse, drug and alcohol addiction. They in turn create non-functional families, compounding the damage. To our great danger, we leave the human, psychological, emotional, spiritual and communal dimensions of life out of our goals, our institutions, and our lives. The same disease occurs on the societal level, where secularism has driven spirit into the extreme defensiveness of fundamentalism.

Restoring the place of the sacred in our lives is essential to healing this disease of the spirit, because it nurtures these very aspects of our relationships whose diminishment has resulted in these seemingly separate problems. In its nurturing of our souls, the sacred is central to sustainability of society and preservation of the ecological health of our planet. And it is the core of a meaningful existence.

To be sustainable, a community must nurture, not neglect, the emotional and spiritual well-being of all. The nature of its work, institutions, and all interactions must nurture self-esteem, mutual respect, and being of value to each other and the community. The principles of equity, security, sustainability, responsibility, giving and sacredness are the healing path for these central diseases of the spirit in growth societies, and living from the heart the way to act upon them.[7]

Healing diseases of the spirit requires bringing spirit back into the heart of our lives and our cultural institutions, including economics. This is not some cloying sugar-coating on our lives, but specific actions to make our work meaningful, our lives rewarding, and our communities conduits of life and well-being. Take the way products are priced in stores, for example:

"Such a commonplace thing, it would be surprising if we did notice. Menus in restaurants. Ads in newspapers. Price tags in grocery stores - even at Goodwill. Yet it is still amazing that we do not rebel, or at least harbor an inner anger, at the oddness those prices truly convey.

I was in a small greengrocer's in Kyoto a couple of years ago when it suddenly struck me how unusual it was that all the prices in that store were in simple round numbers: '500¥ for 200 grams', instead of the '11-3/4 oz. cans for only $3.99' pricing which I'd become accustomed to in grocery stores at home. Simple prices - a gift to make shoppers' decisions easy, in contrast to a trick to cause unwise choices.

It dawned on me then how utterly ubiquitous the value of deceit has become in our society, how frightening our unnoticing acceptance of it is, and how EVERY detail of our lives will need to change to have a society in which we honor each other and work for the good of all."[8]

But now, understanding the diseases of the spirit that arise in the absence of the sacred, we are beginning to understand that a deeper economics rules the attainment of our deeper necessities. Sacred work is essential to our emotional well-being. A sense of the sacredness of life is the only viable alternative to a legalistic, bureaucracy- and rule-bound world. Knowing our continuity of life after death is vital to releasing that great transition from the layers of fear within which many hold it. Experiencing the power of love permits our spirits to soar as nothing else can do.

What constitutes an economics of the sacred? Fairness. Honesty. Honoring others. Joyfulness. Giving. Compassion. Holding the well-being of others and of other life as inviolate as our own. Joining with the rest of Creation to evolve even more wonderful manifestations of the creative impulse behind our universe.

The sacred in our lives and surroundings is essential for personal and social health and survival. Simply put, it deals with "honoring". It deals with respect and reciprocity – with what the Christian Golden Rule distilled into, *"Do unto others as you would have them do unto you."* Honoring the sacred restores us to the wholeness needed to reconnect with our own hearts, our neighbors and the world around us. It give us the strength to summon our vital inner resources and to guide the powerful tools of our technology into right paths.

It teaches us the importance of community- and ecologically-based economics, and of not excluding from our decisions costs passed on to others. It helps us understand the importance of "fair trade," rather than "free trade" whose only freedom is that of exploiting the less powerful. It gives us also the basis for transforming and creating institutions which work to support rather than deplete the lasting supply of world resources, biosystem health, and the capabilities of human and global systems that constitute our real wealth.

All economics, and all cultures and communities derive from distinctive assertions of value. If the values chosen reflect consumption, greed, and violence, they create a far different world than if those values derive from the sacred. E.F. Schumacher, in his path-breaking *Small is Beautiful,*[9] remarked on the characteristic kind of economics which arises from the values of Buddhism – the role and importance of enriching work, of obtaining the maximum well-being from minimum consumption, and of the importance of non-attachment to material wealth. He has shown also its effectiveness in creating successful life, culture, and tools.

Schumacher's "Buddhist" economics is not limited to Buddhists. His insights were seminal in our seeing the distinction between an economics of growth and one of sustainability, an economics of solely material objects and one which enriches the qualities of our lives. Issues of size, of scale and nature of technology, of enduring goods and values, of ownership are all transformed when we set our deepest values as goals of our system of economics.

The pathways by which the sacred affects our lives are many, and sometimes unfamiliar. It affects our bodies in giving us the security of support and nurture by others and obviating the tension of solitary responsibility. It affects our hearts by balancing the ever-present negative emotions of life with the healing and support of love, caring, and being of value. It affects our minds through making visible the positive interactive pathways through which all life cares for us. And it affects our souls through direct connection with the souls of all Creation.

One of the least familiar but most important mechanisms by which our health is affected is through the vehicle of chi or life-force energy, which provides generative and nurturing energy to our lives. *Chi energy turns out to be an important vehicle via which we connect with the sacred and the spirit world, and through which it in turn gives rise to our world and the drama of our lives.*

WORKING *FROM* FULLNESS

A hint of the profound differentness and value of an economy based on energy and spirit can be glimpsed in the words of Malidoma Somé concerning the nature of work in a Dagara community:

> *"Our vision is the starting point of a primal technological power, which is the ability to manifest, to make Spirit real in material form. . . . Spirit and work are linked among indigenous people because human work is viewed as an intensification of the work that Spirit does in nature.*

> *. . . For villagers, the product of any work must be engineered not only to serve the collective good but also to be an extension of the goodness of the collective. For instance, when women get together to make pottery . . . they will begin by chanting and singing together, echoing one another.*

> *. . . They are seated in a circle, and they chant until they are in some sort of ecstatic place, and it is from that place that they begin molding the clay. It is as if the knowledge of how to make pots is not in their brains, but in their collective energy . . . . The women can sit all day in front of two dozen mounds of clay, doing nothing but chanting – until the last hours, when in a flurry of activity all kinds of pots come forth . . . . The product of work here, the pot, embodies the intimacy and wholeness experienced by the women over the course of the day. The women understand that it is necessary to reach that place of wholeness before they can bring something out of it.*

> *. . . Most work in the village is done collectively. The purpose is not so much the desire to get the job done but to raise enough energy for people to feel nourished by what they do. The nourishment does not come after the job, it comes <u>before</u> the job and <u>during</u> the job . . . . You are nourished first, and then the work flows out of your fullness.*

> *. . . As a result of our work practices, the indigenous notion of abundance is very different from that in the West. Villagers are interested not in accumulation but in a sense of <u>fullness</u> . . . . Abundance, in that sense of fullness, has a power that takes us away from worry."*[10]

This process of creating would drive a modern job supervisor crazy. Which is to the point – the work structures we've created are probably unworkable when we are seeking the fuller dimensions and benefits of work.

In the spirit world lies the root of our existence, our purposes, our nurture, and our potentials. Restoring communion between the material and the spirit worlds is vital to the outcome and rightness of all our actions. Sourced in communion with the spirit world, our surroundings and the product of all our actions are permeated with vital energy and rightness of spirit.

Spirit is one of the "unquantifiables" that need to be put first in clarification of any of our decisions. Doing so brings major transformation to our economic practices, and re-opens routes to well-being that require an order-of-magnitude less production of material goods.

---

[1] THE GOLDEN AGE OF CHARTRES, René Querido, Floris Books, 1987.

[2] See SILENCE, SONG & SHADOWS and BUILDING WITH THE BREATH OF LIFE.

[3] For a more details on the role of chi energy in our lives, see BUILDING WITH THE BREATH OF LIFE, Tom Bender, Fire River Press, 2000. On its application in architecture today, also see "Bank of Astoria: Building Community Sustainability," at <www.tombender.org>.

[4] Lomi Lomi, and other energy-based massage techniques, for example. For the role of community ritual, see THE HEALING WISDOM OF AFRICA, Malidoma Somé, Tarcher/Putnam, 1998.

[5] *"The Experimental Verification of Quantum Teleportation,"* NATURE, Dec. 1997; "Scientists Push Quantum Theory Closer to Reality," George Johnson, NYT News Service, Oct.17, '01.

[6] See SILENCE, SONG & SHADOWS, Tom Bender, Fire River Press, 2000, for a more detailed discussion of the role of the sacred in design of our surroundings .

[7] See my HEART OF PLACE, Dec. 1993, for how these manifest in one aspect of society.

[8] *"Simple Prices,"* Tom Bender, FEB. 1996.

[9] SMALL IS BEAUTIFUL, E.F. Schumacher, Harper-Collins 1974, Hartley & Marks, 1999.

[10] THE HEALING WISDOM OF AFRICA, Malidoma Somé, Tarcher/Putnam, 1998.

Chapter 6
Crisis Equals Opportunity

The remarkable achievements of Factor Ten economics may appear value-free. Yet if we look at its origins, they are clearly based in a fundamental shift of values. The seminal *Living Lightly* monograph came directly from an acknowledgment that our welfare is tied with that of all people and all life, and an attempt to change our patterns to make their survival and well-being as possible as our own. Von Weizsächer and Lovins's book, *Factor Four*, begins with a list of *moral* and material reasons for doing more with less – acknowledging that it is in our self-interest to preserve the health of the physical and ecological support systems for humankind. Equity, reducing pollution and depletion of resources, improved quality of life, species extinction and climate change from the greenhouse effect are all given as much prominence as improving efficiency of industrial processes. *Natural Capitalism* gives equal play to ecological and financial benefits.

Initially, the majority of Factor Ten changes have been sought and used to gain competitive advantage, profitability, or market share by private industry. A smaller proportion have resulted in public savings in water rates, energy and material resources. The subtitle to von Weizsäcker and Lovins's *Factor Four – doubling wealth, halving resource use* – is being achieved.

But leaving the benefits of Factor Ten economics to fall largely into higher profits for individuals and businesses is missing the prime opportunity that Factor Ten gives us. We've learned through Factor Ten the importance of optimizing the overall system, not just the subsystem. Aligning our use of the benefits of Factor Ten economics with the values that produced them gives even more direct economic benefits. In addition, it brings ecological, spiritual, security, and success benefits for all.

A GOLDEN OPPORTUNITY

I feel we have a wonderful opportunity – and obligation – to share the benefits from Factor Ten productivity gains with the rest of the world, for several reasons:

> * The insights that have given us the ability to see better ways of doing things did not come from us alone. They came from a network of concerned people working both independently and in concert. They came from the cumulative work of several generations directly, and from several million years of evolution indirectly. As we've benefited from the work of others, others should benefit from ours.

> * Our wealth, and the poverty of others, came in considerable part from economic systems put in place by our ancestors which have drained human and physical resources out of less industrialized nations. That debt should be repaid. "Free trade" is not "fair trade." It supposedly benefits all by allowing the factors of production to move freely to where they can be best applied. It's more than curious, however, that money and material resources are permitted to move freely (*away* from less industrialized countries), but *people* are *prohibited* from moving freely from an area where they are paid 25¢/hour to one where they could be paid $25/hour.

> * The mineral, fossil fuel, forests, soils, and wisdom of many cultures that have been consumed by industrialized cultures are the legacy of the earth to all, and rightfully should be shared equitably.

> * We may question our responsibility for the welfare of others. We do that less, however, if we've ever suffered ourselves. Our family and community is now global, and the same instincts by which we care for members of our individual families apply also to our larger family. From a selfish standpoint, unless we shield ourselves from all life around us, we feel the pain of all. If we are to have either inner peace or national security, all must have well-being.

> * When we are open to spirit, the universe provides for our needs. We are part of that universe for others, and important players in providing for each other *and* for other life.

> * There is no more rewarding or meaningful thing we could do with our lives.

We have an enormous debt to pay – to the poor, to less indus-trialized countries, to other life and our planet – upon whose repay-ment our survival, well-being, and future depend. The elements of an economics of wholeness give the resources and perspectives – if ap-plied today – to bring successful, fulfilling lives to every person on our planet, while restoring ecological balance and evolutionary opportu-nity to all life.

❖

GROWING BETTER, NOT BIGGER

More and more people see our future as untenable – escalat-ing populations already at starvation levels, shrinking water and food resources, depletion of fossil fuels, increasing ecological destruction, climate change and species extinction. Some say there are already far more people than can be supported on a sustainable basis. Some see economic and cultural collapse, war, plague, and mass starvation.

How we deal with growth – in our numbers and in our appe-tites – is central to escaping that forecast of current trends. It's a curi-ous irony that in a profession which has awarded the majority of its Nobel Prizes for work in mathematical analysis, nobody seems willing to address the mathematical impossibility of one of its implicit beliefs – *that growth is unquestionably good*. Though slowing somewhat, world population growth continues exponentially. Any high school math-ematics or biology student can show us that exponential growth can-not continue long in any finite system.

No economic system, however effective, can provide the re-sources unavoidably demanded by continuing exponential growth in our numbers and appetites. Period. We need to acknowledge the ex-ponentially increasing harm that such fantasies are causing, and deal with that root issue up front and directly.

The end result of making continued growth in our population and appetites manageable a little longer is only to place us in a more precarious position a generation from now, with greater numbers, and without the possibility of using resource productivity gains to make a transition to sustainability.

The essential action we need to take *now* is to limit our popu-lation and appetites – in our country and every country. All else is secondary. We'll see below what amazing resources for change that can free. It is also very much in our self-interest to share wealth so that everyone on the planet has the same advantages that we do. That is indispensable for individual, national, and global security.

The economics of wholeness can play a vital role in avoiding the untenable future that projects from our present values and in achieving the most positive future possible. It shows us that:

* *30-40% of our economy goes just to pay the costs of growth.* Stabilizing our numbers and appetites for material goods is vital, and can bring savings of comparable magnitude without loss of quality of life, or even major effort.

* *50% of our economy goes to support inequality.* In the US, inequity of wealth and income is so great that everyone could live as well as the average American, on 50% less production.

* *A 20% surcharge is placed on our costs of living through the use of debt financing.* Reduction in the use of debt produces an equal reduction in income needed.

* *90% (order-of-magnitude) reduction is possible in the economic and resource costs of supplying and operating our institutions,* housing, food production, transportation, and health.

* *More production of material goods is irrelevant to the true goals we seek as individuals and as a culture.*

These are massive potentials, equal to the magnitude required to reach global sustainability.[1]

Our first reaction when someone brings up the issues of depleting resources, rampant ecological damage, or overpopulation is often fear. Fear of "going back to the stone age," of shivering in ragged blankets in a tarpaper shack with an empty stomach. That *might* be a result if we continue to follow traditional habits of thinking and acting. But there are other unexpected and even exciting possibilities in front of us.

If the benefits of economics of wholeness are applied *both* to reducing the impacts of over-industrialized economies and to improving the quality of life in less industrialized economies, we vastly improve the probability of a positive future individual and as a planet.

WHAT DOES GROWTH REALLY COST?

Our present society and the sustainable one which we need to become operate on totally different principles and values. They also generate fundamentally different kinds of costs and rewards as well as immensely different effectiveness in meeting life's needs. Looked at seriously, a sustainable society offers some real surprises compared to our present one. Seeing that its alternatives might be easier and better than expected can help us visualize and approach problems differently.

Let's look a little closer at the possibilities that open up from different perspectives about how we spend money:

1. How much of our work and resources are we spending <u>right now</u> just to pay the demands of <u>growth</u>?

We currently invest immense amounts of our work, energy, and resources to accommodate growth. Every generation, we *double* the number of our houses, cement plants, electrical generating facilities, coal mines, cities, roads, and water systems.[2] We also prematurely demolish overloaded existing facilities to accommodate more people and more "things." And we spend even more educating and feeding those extra people. *This is a significant expenditure, that stabilizing growth totally avoids*.

The cost of growth is significant. It amounts to somewhere between 33% and 40% of our total work.

Avoiding that is equivalent to a gift of 2-3 hours a day, 13-16 hours a week, or 16-21 weeks a year of free time to every person – just for saying NO to more crowding and to jostling for belongings. Choosing not to let our population expand or to have more per capita consumption turns out to hold a massive reward to us as individuals and as a society.

Is it even possible to stabilize growth? The reality is that we've never really tried. The first thing needed is a belief that stabilization is desirable, and a commitment to do it. Period. Other countries have stabilized their populations. China even, has made the more difficult decision to *reduce* its population. Second is to figure out the least intrusive ways of reaching that goal. The only inevitable thing about inevitable growth is that those who would profit from it will try to convince us that growth is inevitable!

Where do we start? Public, personal, and community commitment. Education. Avoiding *unwanted* births. Empowerment of women. Social justice. Economic security and equity. Many believe that these actions alone will achieve a stabilization of population. If more is needed? End subsidies to growth. Stop providing food and medical support of overpopulation. Allow compassionate death. Beyond this, China has shown there are a whole range of further actions which can be successfully used – *if necessary.*

Population and consumption are "commons" issues, but any local jurisdiction can begin the process by stopping subsidy to new development and non-replacement new construction, eliminating tax breaks for relocating industry, freezing urban growth boundaries, capping building permits, requiring evidence of residency for local jobs, eliminating subsidies to large families, taxing wealth rather than homes, and nurturing and encouraging non-material rewards for residents.

There is no way to know with exactness what measures will actually be needed. The essential action is to begin.

2. How much of our work and resources go to pay for <u>inequity</u>?

Another significant share of our resources is used to support inequity in our society. The enormous concentration of wealth by a few in our society consumes vast amounts of resources to benefit only those few. The median US household income for wage-earners is currently $31,000, with more than 13% of households under the monetary poverty level of $15,000. Spreading all that personal income around *equally* would give everyone $59,000 per household.

Or we could support EVERYONE at the <u>current</u> median income level of $31,000 per household. Supporting all households at $31,000/year would need only 53% of currently used work and resources. This would free up almost half of our resources to help others or free our time. Why do we choose to maintain poverty and inequality?

Is achieving equity impossible? It only requires reversing the tax breaks for the wealthy approved over the last 30 years under the belief those tax changes would help *us*! Instead, they have transferred massive amounts of wealth from our pockets to the wealthy, and made us believe our society is suddenly poor. In contrast, Great Britain changed their tax structure *towards* equity after W.W.II, and moved from a far less equal society than ours to one with far greater equity. Finland manages to live quite happily with very little income spread between poor and rich compared to ours.

*Without growth and inequity, <u>every</u> American could live as well as
the average American family does now. At the same time, we
would save <u>two-thirds</u> (67%) of the resources, work, and ecological
damage involved.* And this is without investing a dime in
energy efficiency, improved industrial processes, institutional change, or change in the kind of rewards we get from
life!

3. What would we save just by living on income instead of in <u>debt</u>?

Because of the expense of growth, we have become trapped
into borrowing to pay for personal needs, corporate expansion, and
governmental infrastructure. Our federal government sustains a massive and growing public debt and imbalance of trade. Just the interest
on this debt alone – not even to begin repaying the debt itself – represents a 25% surcharge on other government expenditures. State and
local governments finance virtually all capital improvements – schools,
sewers, hospitals, airports, highways, etc. through selling public bonds.
These result in our ultimately paying double or triple the apparent
cost of those improvements. Interestingly, these costs rarely appear in
discussion of how much is being borrowed.

Our personal finance situations are similar. Interest costs on
home purchases double and triple the actual cost of a home. We finance purchase of one automobile after another for 40 or 50 years, gaining nothing out of the process after the first purchase. (See Endgame
Analysis, Chapter Four) Interest on continuing credit card balances
amounts to over $300 billion per year.

We can't buy any *more* "stuff" by buying on credit. We actually end up being able to buy *less*, because more of our income goes to
paying interest. We just end up *paying more* for what we buy – an
average of 20% more. Here again, consumer debt represents 20% of
disposable income. Corporate debt loads represent a 25% surcharge.
Together, overall debt costs represent more than 20% of our cost of living – a
cost which can be drastically reduced.

Is paying off the federal debt impossible? A one-time, one year
excise tax on the wealthy could pay it off immediately. (That wealth
represents what was left over from having so much income they
couldn't even spend it all.) This would allow federal revenues to return to funding the programs they were intended for rather than paying debt service.

Is cutting the cost of public capital improvements in half impossible? It would only take a requirement for the *repayment* cost of bond issues to be included in advertising of bond issues, and a requirement that public agencies project, prioritize, and pay for capital improvements out of revenues rather than debt. Together, these could cut real financial costs of public capital improvements by more than 50%.

Is radical reduction in our consumer debt and interest costs impossible? Several states already regulate credit card interest rates to within a few percent of prime interest. Japan prohibits carrying a continuous balance on credit card use. Revolving loan funds can eliminate interest costs on home purchases. Car savings plans can encourage savings for purchase rather than paying interest on loan payments. Check out for yourself the difference between using the same monthly payments to *save* to buy cars rather than to *pay* to borrow the same money time after time. And debt costs *more,* and causes serious hardships, in times of deflation and disruption.

TOGETHER, INEQUITY, DEBT, AND GROWTH *QUADRUPLE* OUR COST OF LIVING!

---

4. How much of our work and resources are needlessly wasted on inefficient products and services?

More efficient cars, homes, industrial processes and institutional operation offer incredible magnitudes of savings. As we've seen in previous chapters, well-documented research over the last twenty years is producing *factor of ten* savings (90% reduction) in energy, material, and human resources needed in a vast variety of situations throughout society.

This means 150-200mpg cars – safer than today's, and totally recyclable – due on the road in four to five years. It means homes that require only sunlight and rainfall to operate. Prototypes are already in operation in almost all of our climate zones. Water? Today's appliances already have reduced water use 75% from fixtures only a few years ago – and more improvements are on the way. Forestry practices are available now – requiring no new technology – that maintain *all* forests in old growth condition, while doubling timber production, increasing the economic benefits from timber production nine-fold, and further increasing total forest value.

How about housing that costs only one-tenth of today's, through improved durability, energy efficiency and financing patterns? A higher education system with resources available – *free to all, world-wide* – via satellite TV and Internet? Industrial products with virtually zero ecological impact and a magnitude lower production costs? All these and more are imminent or already being implemented today.

Add these to the benefits of a no-growth, equitable, and debt-free society. That's 10% (Factor Ten) of 80% (avoiding debt) of 50% (equity) of 66% (stabilizing growth) of what we now spend.

With these four changes alone, we would be operating our society at a cost of only 2.6% of what we currently do! That's the equivalent to only working 12 minutes a day to live as well as the average family does now.

It is unlikely that we would ever follow such possibilities out to these extremes – if for no other reason that we decide we *want* to work more, or we *want* to do better for ourselves and all life, and ask for higher levels of performance in all we do. But even if we decide to only achieve two-thirds of each of these savings, that still adds up to an 82% reduction from our present patterns – almost exactly what is projected to be needed to allow everyone on our planet to live with the material benefits that we have, *on a sustainable basis.*

We've looked at these questions very briefly and in isolation. In reality they are interactive. Some give resource savings but not financial or employment ones. Others, as in any ecological system, have multiple and interactive effects and savings. We may choose to work more than twelve minutes a day, but in more rewarding ways. We may choose to do more for others, or create more for ourselves. We will certainly choose different options as we learn the full potentials of the economics of wholeness. What we are showing here is the magnitude of change possible.

What is important is that such simple changes in our values and beliefs of what is possible can totally transform our world.

Accepting growth, inequity, debt, or inefficient economics just because we are accustomed to them, or because a beneficiary tells us they are essential, is no longer acceptable. Each of them has extraordinary costs, and would require extraordinary justification to continue.

UNEXPECTED GIFTS

We find unexpected bonuses when we try on the unthinkable – a world which seeks *better* rather than *bigger*, a world where growth in *quality* replaces growth in numbers and material goods.[3]

As we've seen, instead of just maintaining what we have to meet the needs of our present population, growth has required that we build from scratch every generation entirely new facilities to house and feed twice as many people. Without that population growth, we can avoid our need for all that work and resource use, and use it to help others.

"Qualitative growth" means dramatically lessened impact on resources, farm land, and each other. It means less work and more leisure for everyone. It means resources can be available to deal with real needs.

It means time for sports, music, community, art, games and leisure - both inside and out of work. Without the belief that we have to be continuous and excessive consumers to keep our economy afloat, it means we can find personal freedom from debt, from stress of work and consumption, and the burden of unneeded "things."

Without "growth" as an excuse ("there will be more for everyone") to keep from dealing with issues of equity, we will face and be able to deal with those issues which underlie so many of our social problems. With that, the fears which have increasingly filled our lives can be resolved.

Living from values that we can be proud of allows us to speak from the heart. It lets us live life with an open heart; reconnect and share energy with others; and permits the life and wisdom of others to add measure to our own. Our everyday actions begin to reveal new senses of the universe we inhabit.

CAN WE CHANGE THE WORLD?

Can such benefits be used to help people globally? Let's look at a couple of examples of what is currently in the works, or already accomplished, and how the conviction that major change is possible can help us see that simple changes in our values can open extraordinary opportunities.

STRAWBALE HOUSING IN CHINA AND MEXICO

Bringing together the wisdom of very different cultures can *and already is* providing dramatic order-of-magnitude improvements in basic needs such as housing. Straw bale building construction is one of the new and simple building technique which have developed over the last ten years, based on ecological values, global needs, and a desire for success for all. Taking a frequently wasted agricultural product with low cost and high insulating potential, natural-building advocates have developed a construction process with unique potentials for the dry and often cold prairie lands where the straw comes from.

Architect Kelly Learner, Scott Christiansen and a team of straw-bale builders have been teaching straw-bale construction in Mongolia, China, and South America for the last several years, in conjunction with organizations such as the Adventist Development Relief Agency and the United Nations Development Program. Groups working with them have built health clinics, schools, houses, and other facilities.

One project in China in the summer of 2000 built fifteen houses in one village and ten in another, with a construction cost of a little over $2000/house ($3.75/sq.ft.). In an area where winter temperatures plummet to -40^0, straw-bale has reduced construction costs by 20%, coal use and CO_2 and particulate emissions by 80%. At the same time these houses have provided dramatic increase in comfort for their residents – raising winter interior temperatures from just above freezing to about 65-70^{0}F. As an important bonus, these houses employ simple but sophisticated engineering design to allow them to survive the major earthquakes experienced in the region.

The same families previously spent 30-50% of their income on heating coal. Straw bale construction has achieved 80% reduction in heating costs, while improving comfort and well-being. It has freed 25-40% of family income for other priority needs, reduced demands on natural resources, and lessened resultant pollution from the burning of coal by an equal 80%. No wonder there is already a waiting list of 1000 families in one county in China alone, and plans in that small part of China to build 10,000 straw-bale homes over the next 3-4 years![4]

In community facilities, UNDP found Mongolia rural social service providers were spending more than 50% of their budgets on heating fuel. With passive solar straw-bale construction reducing heating bills by 50-75%, schools and clinics can now provide better services to more people. This has already led to a $2 million UNDP project to build 90 social services buildings in rural communities.[5]

Courtesy DSA Architects

Strawbale farm worker housing, with softly tinted clay plaster and hand-made ornament by the owners, shows that even simple and inexpensive buildings can be beautiful, fit their surroundings, and move our hearts.

In Sonora, Mexico, Athena and Bill Steen's Canelo Project[6] has been teaching women to build their own straw bale houses, and community groups to build schools, churches and public buildings. Their spirited use of simple local materials, natural clay plasters, pigments, and adobe floors has shown that astonishing beauty is possible with such simple means and that every community has the means to surround itself with beauty.

RESOURCE EFFICIENT APPLIANCES

A similar, virtually unnoticed, revolution has taken place in home appliance efficiency, allowing developing countries to leap-frog resource efficiency as such products come into more widespread use:

* New refrigerator designs reducing electrical use from a 350kwh average in 1988 to about 30kwh.

* Clothes washers and dryers using 40-75% less water, 90% less electricity for hot water and washing, and through better detergents and higher-speed spin cycles reducing electricity use for drying by fifty percent.

* $13 shower heads that reduce water use (and water heating energy) by seven-fold.

* Low-flush toilets (already in use in Japan in 1965) using 1-1.5 gallons per flush instead of 5-7 gallons; "dual flush" design to allow even greater water savings when flushing just liquids; optional triangular tanks which allow toilets to be installed in corners, saving more space; and with a sink installed in the tank lid for hand washing, storing hand-washing water in the tank for reuse in flushing the toilet.

* Waterless toilets and urinals which cost no more than conventional toilets, require no water or sewers, and make nutrients available again for food production.

* Cookstoves that reduce electrical use two-thirds, and microwave ovens that reduce energy use even more.

* Compact, dimmable fluorescent light bulbs with electronic ballast, as versatile as incandescent bulbs, while producing 3-4 times the light per watt of electricity.[7]

Many countries are beginning to look at energy and resource use in a more comprehensive way, seeing the interconnection between different actions and choices. They are realizing that building factories to make *high-efficiency* appliances *avoids the need* to construct and operate four out of five power-generating plants that would otherwise be required, compounding the savings.

HIGHER EDUCATION

There is no consensus that the industrialized nations' model of sixteen years or more of predominantly intellectual, literacy-centered education is wise. But it is sought after, and considerable human and economic resources are committed to its attainment. A shift in the pattern of achieving it can open the process to become more multidimensional, while providing Factor Ten reductions in cost and making it globally accessible.

Institutional performance is as adaptable to Factor Ten improvements as is energy efficiency of transportation systems or the performance of our buildings. Higher education provides a good example of potentials for institutional change, of the incredible magnitude of improvement possible where information is a prime element being dealt with, and of how we can make improvements available globally at extremely low cost.

The basic structure of our higher education system has been unchanged since before the printing press was invented, when teachers were the sole source of learning content. An estimated two-thirds of undergraduate credit hours uses a classroom lecture-style structure. In it an instructor covers virtually the same material as in the texts used. The same coverage is repeated by other instructors in other sections, other years, and other institutions. This redundancy is amazingly wasteful of both faculty and financial resources, as well as student time.

There are at least four major goals of our higher education systems:[8]

* Access to learning resources
* Accrediting learning achievement
* Job competency certification
* Research

These are today interwoven in an instructor-centered, course-based system, in which light faculty workloads underwrite major free time for personal research; individual faculty do testing of student achievement; course requirements are prescribed for degrees giving access to specific fields of work; a lecture-centered system provides very expensive redundancy of learning resources; and faculty are hired based on expertise in their field of work, not competency in teaching, testing, research, or certification.

Looking at those major goals and asking what more direct paths might exist to achieve them, we find that accreditation, certification, and research can be handled far more effectively through other means. Discussion and tutoring can be handled in a variety of ways locally within the educational communities. Access to learning resources is probably the most important element, usually composed of books and lectures. Books are relatively cheap, and can be made virtually free electronically, or through sharing via libraries.

Lectures, administrative overheads, and facilities are a huge cost. If we think of only one lecture course given only twice a year in only four colleges in each of fifty states, we have 400X redundancy at a cost of $5 million/year in the U.S. alone. Compare that to the cost of videotaping the lectures and making them available via satellite and Internet to everyone in the world. Over ten years, in just twenty countries, that would amount to $1 billion redundancy *per course* – just for the lecturing – that could be released to other uses. The human and economic resources that could be freed for better use are staggering.

This is only one element in a viable higher education system, but arguably the most expensive, and the most easily transformed. More comprehensive details for opening up and restructuring higher education are found in Appendix D. In aggregate they still attain far more than a Factor Ten improvement in resource productivity, while providing global access to user-initiated learning.

Potentials for greater productivity in information, higher education, and electronic communication are fairly easy for us to grasp. *Factor Four* similarly documents savings in excess of 99% in energy and material resources (not to mention time) for a six-hour trans-Atlantic videoconference replacing holding the same meeting in a single location. Such alternatives can dramatically lower the cost to others of accessing the kind of education that we have valued. And they can equally give us opportunity to make contact with the very different wisdom of other cultures.

The savings from an economics of wholeness are immense. Even if we just share the *savings* with others, we can change the world.

---

[1] *"It's Oil Right, Folks! There's Good Times Ahead,"* Tom Bender, SOLAR ENERGY ASSOCIATION OF OREGON, 1996.

[2] See *"It's Oil Right, Folks!"* above. For community growth subsidies, see BETTER, NOT BIGGER," Eben Fodor, New Society, 1999; and publications of Alternatives to Growth Oregon, <www.AGOregon.org>.

[3] from *"Shedding A Skin That No Longer Fits,"* Tom Bender, Mar. 1996. Reprinted in IN CONTEXT, July 1996.

[4] THE LAST STRAW, Issue #33, Spring 2001, p34-35.

[5] ALTERNATIVE CONSTRUCTION, Lynne Elizabeth and Cassandra Adams, ed., John Wiley & Sons, 2000. P339-356.

[6] THE BEAUTY OF STRAW BALE HOMES, Athena and Bill Steen, Chelsea Green, 2001.

[7] FACTOR FOUR, above; LIVING LIGHTLY, above; ENVIRONMENTAL BUILDING NEWS, etc.

[8] Excerpted from *"Vitality and Affordability of Higher Education,"* Tom Bender, Oct. 1993, as part of State of Oregon review of Higher Education. Republished in IN CONTEXT, July 1996.

Chapter 7
Tools for Whole-Systems Economics

The most important tools for capturing the benefits of economics of wholeness are those in our minds and hearts. They help us gain different perspectives which generate significantly better alternatives. Appendix A contains a summary list of these tools that can be copied to keep handy as a checklist:

I. ROOT GOALS

* WORK WITH SPIRITUAL FRAMEWORKS AND ECONOMIC SYSTEMS WHICH ARE CONGRUENT
> Every specific economic system enables and disables different root values. Every spiritual framework is best embodied in a unique economic system.

* SEEK *REAL* WEALTH
> Our real wealth is a lasting supply of world resources, biosystem health, and the capabilities of human and global systems. They define the boundaries of the possible.[1]

> * A WEALTHY WORLD is one with:
> > – A healthy and growing diversity of lifeforms, communities and capabilities. They are our stockpile of potential.
> * A WEALTHY COMMUNITY is one with:
> > – A meaningful sense of its place in the universe.
> > – A healthy and growing diversity of capabilities, individuals and lifeforms.
> > – A satisfying spiritual, emotional and material heritage, life, and prospect.

* A WEALTHY INDIVIDUAL is one with:
    – The love and respect of others, the ability to give.
    – Equitable opportunity for the physical, emotional and spiritual health which the natural world can sustain.
    – Opportunity to develop and employ innate capabilities and to be of real value to the community.

* MEET GLOBAL NEEDS WITH WASTED RESOURCES
    The magnitude of resources wasted today can make the lives of everyone a success.

* ACHIEVE EQUITY OF WEALTH ESSENTIAL TO FULFILLMENT OF POTENTIALS
    Significant inequity of wealth generates inequity of power, which almost inevitably blocks the potentials of the less powerful and generates social problems.

* ENSURE SUSTAINABILITY
    If we can't ensure tomorrows at least as good as today, we're stealing from our children.

* SEEK *WISDOM*, NOT INFORMATION; SHARE KNOWLEDGE WITH ALL
    It is cheaper to *give* information away than to manage control of it. Multi-lingual global information access can give a 25 to 50-fold decrease in the cost of higher education.[2]

* REPLENISH NATURAL SYSTEMS
    Restoring the health and productivity of over-exploited soils, forests, fisheries, agricultural lands, water and energy resources can provide astounding economic returns as well as improving the sustainability base of our communities.[3]

* DON'T LOSE WHAT WE CAN'T REPLACE
    Maximize energy and material productivity, renewable energy use, and material recycling. Preserve bio-diversity, and the wisdom of all cultures.

* DON'T NEED IT – DON'T FIGHT FOR IT
    Reducing resource competition underlying global discord frees military dollars to be used to heal people and places. Reducing vulnerability to terrorism is tied to lessening globalized economic dependencies.[4]

* AVOID NEEDS
> It is far cheaper to avoid the need for services than to supply them, however efficiently. REAL wealth is *not needing* transportation, health care or other institutional services.

* HONOR THE TRADITIONAL WISDOM OF ALL CULTURES
> Diversity is richness. Different cultures and traditions create different realities and different potentials. Knowing and acknowledging their value underlies the mutual respect needed for sustainable relations.

* LOOK FOR THE *REAL* REWARDS WE SEEK
> Such rewards are usually spiritual, emotional, and psychological, and often better attained outside of material systems.

* BUILD ON SUSTAINABLE VALUES
> The values necessary for sustainability invoke a better, and very different, way of life:[5]

> - PERMANENCE instead of profit
> - PEOPLE instead of professions
> - RESPONSIBILITIES instead of rights
> - ENOUGHNESS instead of moreness
> - AUSTERITY instead of affluence
> - BETTERMENT instead of biggerment
> - LOCALIZATION instead of centralization
> - WORK instead of leisure
> - EQUITIZATION instead of urbanization
> - TOOLS instead of machines

> When our minds change, changes in our actions follow with little effort.

* SEEK SPIRITUAL CONNECTION WITH OUR SURROUNDINGS, OTHER CULTURES, AND NATURAL SYSTEMS
> Peace, harmony and meaning – with our dreams, with our neighbors, and with our surroundings – are crucial to any community.

* PROVIDE THE WEALTH OF REWARDING WORK
> Maximize work which rewards and enriches the skills of the worker. Use technology as *tools* rather than machines. The most important product of work is in the worker.

* CHOOSE ACTIONS AND ECONOMICS THAT SUSTAIN OUR RELATION WITH OTHER PEOPLE AND THE REST OF LIFE

How we provide for our needs is a carrier of these less tangible dimensions even more important than the obvious product itself.

* TOUCH THE SPIRIT OF WHERE WE LIVE

The uniqueness of a region creates a special culture and community once we come to feel at home in it. Learning to value and celebrate that specialness is necessary to a region's sustainability, to effective matching of resources and needs, and to our own comfort and enjoyment.[6]

* CONNECT US WITH THE STARS

We are their children and kin. So is all life on our planet. A true sense of our place in the universe must underlie any living community. The universe we inhabit is more awe-inspiring than any traditional myth, and new avenues are opening to make contact with it. Honoring these connections in making our surroundings acknowledges our place in the whole incredible dance of the universe.

* NURTURE INNER RESOURCES

The power of our minds and spirits surpasses even that of our technology. Those inner resources need shelter, nurture, challenge and opportunity for engagement. We need ways to powerfully stimulate our inner resources and connect them with the wonders of the world around us.

* CREATE PLACES FOR OUR HEARTS AND MINDS

Working in new information-intensive environments is bringing us to again appreciate the need for their counter-point – quietly evocative environments where we can assimilate, process, and integrate that information into creative and effective action.

* SEEK WHAT DRAWS FORTH LOVE

Love, in more than a metaphorical sense, is what both fuels and binds the universe and our dreams, and its experience is one of the root goals we seek with our lives.

* GIVE THE UNEXPECTED

Love is expressed in our willingness to give without condition. The most precious thing we can convey is a sense of unstinted giving – of doing something out of love rather than calculation. Giving initiates a reciprocity that grows in value to both the giver and receiver.

* EMBRACE THE SACREDNESS OF ALL CREATION

> Diseases of the spirit are the root illness of our time. Most intractable social problems arise out of lack of self-worth, lack of respect by and for others, or lack of opportunity to be of use and value to family and society. They are all a disease of the spirit.

* HONOR LIFE, AND THE POWER THAT BEGETS IT

> The forms and forces of life are primary. Our possessions are of far less import. Ask anyone who has escaped tragedy with their lives and those of their loved ones. Ask what truly gives joy and for what the future will thank us.

* GIVE OUR SPIRITS HOMES

> They need shelter and nourishment as well as our bodies. That nourishment creates our wealth, and is the glue that holds sustainability and well-being together

* HONOR THINGS

> Tradition honors the insights of the past. Planting trees honors hope for a future. A tokonoma honors guests. Providing place for birds to nest honors the other lives that share our world. Honoring the past lives of building materials makes us aware of the beauty and struggles of all life.

* CONNECT US TO THE LIFE AROUND US

> This does not require large budgets or spaces. It needs only the desire for that connection and a willingness to evolve a life and surroundings that are unique.

II. PREPARING OURSELVES

* ASSUME WE REALLY DON'T KNOW WHAT WE'RE DOING

> Most of what we do does not come from deep knowledge of what we're trying to do. We can assume that going deeper can reveal productive insights. Remember the Chinese adage, "The Third Pig Is Always Fattest."[7]

* WORK FROM A CONVICTION THAT WE CAN ACHIEVE *MAGNITUDES* OF CHANGE

> What you don't believe, you won't achieve.

* THINK INTEGRATIVELY AND ECOLOGICALLY
Everything is part of a multidimensional web of relationships. Awareness of total interactions must be basis of
actions and changes.

* THINK OUTSIDE OF THE BOX
"The box" is a measure of previous limits. If we can see the
box, we can see what's outside of it.

* ASSUME ANYTHING THAT COMES TO MIND CAN BE PART OF
A POTENTIAL SOLUTION
Our minds work better than we understand, and they have
open phone lines to the rest of Creation. When something,
however odd, comes to mind, figure out what it might
contribute.

* EXAMINE MULTIPLE-REWARD SYSTEMS, SUCH AS GIVING AND
SHARING
Giving rewards both the giver and the receiver. Sharing has
multiple benefits. Many other patterns have multiple
benefits that need to be accounted.

* BREAK RULES
Rules are something we've imposed on a situation to contain
it. Yesterday's pattern of containment may not be appropriate for tomorrow.

* USE LATERAL AND BRIDGE THINKING
Consider how advances in other fields can apply to the
one under consideration.

* LOOK FOR THE *HEART* ISSUES BENEATH THE *HEAD* ONES
Many of the fears and uncertainties deepest in our hearts are
hard to talk about. Issues we *do* raise often obscurely reflect
those deeper questions. Look for the openings to resolve
root problems.

* REMEMBER THAT GOAL AND PROCESS ARE ONE
The path, and how it is walked, *is* often the goal. A good
goal does not justify a bad process. We can't talk of technique in the abstract.

* REPLACE MATERIAL AND ENERGY RESOURCES
WITH INSIGHT AND INGENUITY
Brute force is expensive.

* TOUCH THE HEART OF ALL WE MAKE

>   Sustainable actions are not effective without clarity of purpose. Such clarity often transfers the initiative from the institution to the individual, and employ more effective and empowering interactive patterns.

* EXPERIENCE CHI ENERGY

>   Anything outside the familiar is abstract until experienced. Life-force energy plays a vital role in how our universe works, which we need to understand and incorporate in our decisions.

III. INTEGRATED SYSTEMS DESIGN

* *AVOID* PROBLEMS RATHER THAN SOLVE THEM

>   It costs less not to have a problem to deal with than to resolve one.

* LOOK FOR BIG CHANGES IN PATTERNS, NOT FINE-TUNING OF EXISTING ELEMENTS

>   Many small changes can cost far more to achieve than a single large one. Different patterns may have far different attributive costs. We've already looked for small improvements, but not for *big* ones.

* BUILD FOR ETERNITY

>   Durability in mature capital goods rewards handsomely, and grants a generosity not otherwise possible. In consumable goods, durability often wastes resources. Planning for 1000-year lives of our buildings and communities ensures we pay attention to long term effects of our actions.

* FIND ACTIONS THAT YIELD MULTIPLE BENEFITS

>   Find ways to link the beneficiaries to support the action.

* REMEMBER PRINCIPLES OF SUSTAINABLE SYSTEMS ARE OFTEN THE INVERSE OF GROWTH SYSTEMS

>   The opposite of the familiar may work better when changing systems. Observe when it is prudent to switch from one to the other.

* MINIMIZE TRUE LIFECYCLE COSTS

> Evaluate for the user's lifecycle as well as for product's lifecycle. Include cradle to grave costs – extraction, embodied, capital, operating, maintenance, institutional, and restoration costs.

* KNOW THE *TRUE* COSTS

> Economic rather than financial costing shows the real effects of our actions and choices:[8]

>> – Externalized costs – current and future impacts on other natural and technical systems.

>> – Institutional performance – including no-build means of reaching policy objectives.

>> – Energy / material resource performance.

>> – Monetary cost - including lifecycle costs, financing costs, and residual value.

>> – Comparative value as a social investment; contribution and costs to social systems.

* *ASSUME* ROOM FOR ORDER-OF-MAGNITUDE IMPROVEMENT IN ANY SYSTEM NOT PREVIOUSLY EXAMINED

> Wealthy societies inevitably generate inefficient institutions – it is often easier to throw money at symptoms than to deal with root problems.

* SEEK SOLUTIONS INCREASING SECURITY AND STABILITY

> Instability can generate immense externalized costs. Imposed security is illusionary and expensive.

* LET NATURE DO IT

> Use natural systems. Use natural processes. Let nature provide complex subsystems. The productivity of natural systems is profound.

* FIND THE PRIMARY GOALS OF THE SYSTEM

> Then examine other ways – inside *and* outside of the system, together *and* separately – of attaining them.

* SEEK SOLUTIONS SATISFYING TO *ALL* INVOLVED
> Any other solutions will be continually contested and undermined. Consensus agreement is essential for enthusiasm, involvement and unfolding maximum potentials.

* FOCUS ON SERVICE FLOWS, NOT PRODUCT
> Providing service, not product, internalizes operational and maintenance costs within a primary beneficiary.

* VIEW POLLUTION OR WASTE PRODUCTS AS *RESOURCES* OUT OF PLACE
> Both are concentrated resources, with potential profitable uses.

* ELIMINATE PROFIT
> Competition in theoretical mature economic systems eliminates unearned income. Basing acceptable returns in mature or regulated industries on those in emerging fields overvalues those investments.

* ACKNOWLEDGE WHAT YOU SEE
> Include what *you* see as a true cost of a system, even if conventional accounting doesn't. The accounting system is as likely to be in error as you are.

* DON'T ACCEPT ECONOMIC, ACCOUNTING, AND REGULATORY CONVENTIONS
> Conventions, such as "present-value accounting," are *tactical* tools, worth using only when their results justify their use. Factor Ten approaches which violate such conventions often produce benefits of such magnitudes that it becomes obvious that the use of traditional conventions should not apply.

IV. ECOLOGICAL SYSTEM CHARACTERISTICS

* CLOSE LOOPS
> Find the cycles as well as the flows through the systems involved. If closed cycles are missing, so is sustainability.

* OPTIMIZE EMBRACING SYSTEMS RATHER THAN EMBEDDED ONES
> The value of embedded systems includes what they contribute to the embracing system, not just their own existence.

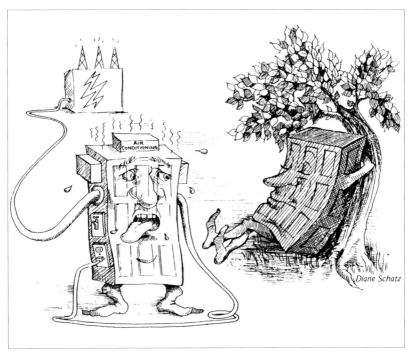

One tree equals a dozen room air conditioners. Avoiding problems, letting nature do it, and using natural systems are all concepts that apply to a variety of personal, institutional, and production issues.

The value of a building that improves occupant productivity is greater than one that merely minimizes its own costs.

* TRACK THE ENERGY FLOWS

Energy flows, qualities and transformations in a system give vital information on how it works and how to change it. Minimize material resource and depletable energy use. Cascade energy uses.

* LOOK AT EXPENDITURES AS *COSTS*

Seen from a larger system, expenditures on the product of the subsystem being examined are *costs*, which are to be minimized, not sales to be maximized.

* LOOK FOR THE MULTIPLE ELEMENTS WHICH MAKE UP TRUE SOLUTIONS TO ANY PROBLEM

There is rarely a single cause of any problem, nor a single solution that works.

* SEEK SOLUTIONS THAT SOLVE MULTIPLE PROBLEMS
     Elements of ecological systems perform multiple functions.
     Those multiple benefits need to be accounted.

* USE ECOLOGICAL ECONOMICS (1+1=3)
     Account for the values of complexity.

* AVOID INTERMEDIARIES
     They often disrupt information flow and feedback, and add
     cost to the system.

* CONSIDER ADDING INTERMEDIARIES
     Feeding birds to spread their seeds is a more productive
     survival strategy for some plants. Complexity can give
     stability.

V. FINE TUNING

* REMEMBER LOVINS' "GET THE SEQUENCE RIGHT":
     – People before hardware
     – Shell before contents
     – Application before equipment
     – Quality before quantity
     – Passive before active
     – Load reduction before supply
     – Optimize the whole, not the parts
     – Start downstream to turn compounding losses into savings

* SEEK PATTERNS THAT *ELIMINATE* NEED FOR OTHER ELE-
MENTS
     Solutions not cost-effective in themselves may yield
     great benefit if they allow elimination rather than
     reduction of another element.

* EFFICIENCY IN *IMPORTANT* THINGS IS MORE SIGNIFICANT
THAN IN UNIMPORTANT THINGS
     The inner product of work – what happens to us, and our
     relations to others and to other things in the process – is
     more important than the outer products.[9]

* USE *DISTRIBUTED* INTELLIGENCE AND RESPONSIBILITY IN A
SYSTEM
     What's close at hand is better known and cared for.

* MINIMIZE SECONDARY AND MANAGERIAL WORK

> They are a sign of oversize, over-complicated, and feedback-poor systems.

* AVOID SIZE WHERE POSSIBLE

> Size usually entails information, transportation, management, and other avoidable costs.

* MAKE WHERE WE *ARE* PARADISE!

> Making what we have enjoyable is simpler than seeking enjoyment elsewhere.

* REINVENT WHAT EXISTS

> Innovative recycling of auto-centered communities can save our investment in them and give them productive new lives.

* LOOK FOR SOLUTIONS THAT TAKE ADVANTAGE OF LOCAL CONDITIONS

> Intimate knowledge gives sensitive responses.

* AVOID AND COUNTER EFFECTS OF ADVERTISING

> Micro-breweries succeed through word-of-mouth "discovery."

* LIVE SIMPLY, WORK LESS

> Solutions that *free* time may be more valuable than ones that provide new opportunities to use time.

* AVOID SOLUTIONS THAT TRANSFER RATHER THAN REDUCE COSTS

> Passing the buck doesn't make things more productive. It only makes others pay the cost.

* REPLACE MATERIAL AND ENERGY RESOURCES AND WORK WITH INFORMATION

> Information's cheap.

* REPLACE INFORMATION WITH WISDOM

> What *can* be done isn't the same as what *should* be done.

Diane Schatz

Discounting the future, eating our seed corn, not worrying about tomorrow, become self-fulfilling prophecies. Maximizing what we have now inevitably reduces what we have for tomorrow. Yesterday's now-centeredness has already decreased what we have available today.

PENNY WISE AND POUND FOOLISH?

Our existing economics has focused almost exclusively on short-term thinking. Through a variety of practices, such as "present value accounting" (PNV), it has ignored and discounted the real future results of alternative courses of action, and ignored the vital importance of long-term and unquantifiable benefits.

There are many internal inconsistencies and conceptual errors in such approaches, which I will ignore here. As we've seen from a variety of examples, Factor Ten economics has conclusively shown two things:

* We are *always* in the "long-term" as well as the "short-term." End-game analysis (chapter four) shows that strikingly different results occur when we examine the long-

term as well as short-term results of our actions. Short-term viewpoints are tactical – means of transitioning from present positions to desired long-range positions. If carried out repeatedly or over a prolonged period, their results are usually highly counterproductive. Long-term strategies provide maximum benefits. The earlier we apply them, the greater our rewards.

* Whatever the internal logic of PNV and similar practices, in practice they fail by an order-of-magnitude in comparison with Factor Ten economics.[10] The value of a tool is measured by what it can achieve. The bottom line is important, and we've been looking at the *wrong* bottom line. Compared to Factor Ten economics, they fail so badly that they no longer have credibility, and should not rate further consideration.

OMISSIONS OF CONVENTIONAL ECONOMICS

This might be a good place to summarize some of the ways that conventional economics, in spite of its many successes, has failed to keep visible the true costs of options before us:

* Ignoring the mathematical impossibility (and exponentially increasing costs) of continued exponential growth of population and material goods in finite ecological systems.

* Excluding or "discounting" future benefits.

* Using welfare indicators such as GNP and stock market indexes that omitted major sectors of the economy such as unpaid family work, that valued turnover rather than stocks of goods, and that gave false indicators of actual well-being of individuals and society. An indicator that counts expenses as income inevitably gives the wrong signals.

* Using analytical tools biased towards short-term rather than long-term benefits.

* Neglecting to see costs of "diseases of the spirit" generated by our economic system.

* Considering higher expenditures to be equivalent to better quality of life gained.

* Failure to separate economic from financial analyses.

* Failure to include debt service costs in public "debt-financing" ballot issues and budgeting.

* Ignoring significantly different costs of *repeated* actions such as debt-financing or "bond issues."

* Omitting multiple costs and benefits of alternative actions – focusing solely on primary "engineering" goals.

* Externalizing and ignoring costs passed on to others.

* Developing systems that maximize, rather than minimize, profit.

* Focusing on obtaining material objects as supposed equivalent of attaining personal and cultural goals.

* Confusing durable vs. consumable wealth; material vs. immaterial benefits.

* Focusing on supplying wants rather than reducing needs.

* Optimizing embedded systems rather than embracing systems.

* Using death-centered rather than life-centered approaches to medicine, food, etc. that breed drug- and pesticide-resistant "super-bugs."

This is not to "blame" conventional economics. It has accomplished many wonderful things. But seeing why it consistently has missed desirable options and chosen more detrimental ones can help us see where it got off course and help us avoid repeating the same errors.

Try these tools, and see how they can help you find new perspectives. Don't discount the future – the rest of our lives, those of our children, and all the rest of history resides there.[11]

[1] See *"Building Real Wealth,"* Tom Bender, May. 1993, for details on subsequent items. Text of top award winning entry in International Sustainable Community Solutions Competition, 1993. Reprinted in IN CONTEXT, Issue 44, July, 1996.

[2] See *"Vitality and Affordability of Higher Education,"* Tom Bender, Oct. 1993. Reprinted in IN CONTEXT, July 1996.

[3] See the State of California's highly successful *"Investing for Prosperity"* program.

[4] See "True Security," "The End of Nuclear War," above. Also, BRITTLE POWER: Energy Strategy for National Security, Amory and L. Hunter Lovins, Brick House, 1982; SECURITY WITHOUT WAR, Hal Harvey and Mike Shuman, Westview, 1993.

[5] See Appendix B for more detailed discussion of these sustainable values.

[6] See *"Northern Lights,"* Tom Bender, WINTER CITIES FORUM, 1986.

[7] *"The Third Pig Is Always Fattest,"* Tom Bender, RAIN Magazine, May, 1977.

[8] *BUILDING VALUE,* Tom Bender, Office of California State Architect, 1976.

[9] *"Technology is Not the Problem and Not the Answer"*, RAIN, May, 1977.

[10] *"Improving the Economic Value of Coastal Public Forest Lands,"* Tom Bender, Dec. 1994; IN CONTEXT, July 1996.

[11] For more detailed discussion, see *"Sharing Smaller Pies,"* Tom Bender, 1975; reprinted in RAIN Magazine, April '75 and Oct. '83; New Age Journal, Nov. '75; THE FUTURIST, 1976; RESETTLING AMERICA, Gary Coates, ed., 1981; UTNE READER, Fall, 1987. Also, *"Building Real Wealth,"* above; *"Tunneling through the Cost Barrier,"* Amory Lovins, RMI Newsletter, Summer 1997; "Beyond Natural Capitalism," Lovins and Hawken, <www.natcap.org>.

Chapter 8
Governance and Community

The intent of this chapter is not to provide a detailed recipe for legislation to implement economics of wholeness. Most of that is happening already in the marketplace, governmental actions need to be arrived at by a process of consensus, and there is not space here to detail proposals so they don't appear utopian. What we *can* do here is:

* Look at government and community as an example of applying some of the tools discussed in the previous chapter.

* Examine some policy actions already implemented by various governmental jurisdictions to bring the "game rules" of the marketplace in line with economics of wholeness.

GOVERNANCE IS NOT GOVERNMENT

We're used to considering government being the same thing as governance, and of economics being the transactions between production firms and consumers. The real world, however, is not that simple, and is becoming more complex every day. The Federal Government theoretically manages the money supply. But what happens when private credit card companies suddenly unleash a massive electronic equivalent of money onto the market? Center-pivot irrigation dramatically changes land prices in many agricultural areas – until the underground aquifer is depleted. Decisions within a household affect money and resource flow as well as demands for products and services, and where satisfactions are sought.

There are many more players in the interactive process of either governance or economics than our simplified models normally account for. In economics, there is built capital, social capital, human capital and natural capital as well as monetary capital. All, and the interactions of all, need to be accounted for. Not only governments, but Non-Governmental Organizations (NGOs), multi-national corporations, media, religious groups and individuals have leverage in achieving effectively political decisions. All are part of the embracing system in which economics is embedded.

While it seems sometimes that "someone else" has all the power to make decisions, it should be very apparent today that actions of a few individuals can totally transform predictions. Banking mergers appeared to head the banking industry into dominance by a handful of firms – until customers started to leave the mega-banks in droves for community banks. Nuclear power looked to be the future for generating electricity – until individual energy efficiency choices, at a fraction of the cost, took the market away. Changes in geographic organization, hierarchy, economic base, information access, and beliefs are occurring with increasing rapidity, transforming the substructure of our economic system.

It isn't government, and it isn't economists, that have been bringing about the transformations of Factor Ten economics to date. It is the creative leaders of industry that are transforming business practices. It is environmentalists and energy efficiency engineers that are transforming resource productivity. And it is our individual decisions of what work is rewarding to us, what purchasing patterns are deceptive, what quality of food we want to eat that are bringing value changes to the marketplace. They are the forces on the planet that are well managed enough and resourceful enough to solve the problems facing us. Governance is a multi-faced interactive "driving-system" for a culture, one which is more open than we imagine to individual action. Even just asking some new questions, or not accepting some old answers can lead to major change.

❖

FACTOR TEN PUBLIC POLICY
Government jurisdictions are public institutions, with less incentive towards leanness than private ones, and with continual imposition of new and often conflicting laws and regulations. Even without the potentials of new economics, there is need for periodic overhaul, renewal, and refocusing. The tools developed in previous chapters can be applied successfully to government agency performance and impact on productivity – the student housing analysis discussed below achieved an 80% reduction in costs in a public policy decision merely by fuller inclusion of the true costs of alternatives. Aligning

public policy with resource productivity can provide key leverage for widespread capture of its economic benefits.

Taxes

The U.S. Internal Revenue Service has become an impenetrable labyrinth of complicated special-interest tax legislation. Record-keeping and tax filing takes an increasing cut of taxpayer's time, in addition to frustration and increasing inequity.

Several organizations working with resource productivity have made a strong case for totally abolishing the IRS and starting over with a tax system that taxes "bads" rather than "goods." Taxing extraction of oil and minerals, rather than giving depletion tax *credits*, leads to more efficient use of the resources, prolongs their availability, and encourages rather than inhibits recycling. Taxing pollution rather than the purchase of goods encourages better use of those wasted resources as well as reducing pollution-caused health and ecological damages. Changing from our current tax of income to taxing resource use encourages employment rather than resource depletion.

During the 1974 oil supply crisis, all sorts of complex and cumbersome regulatory proposals were proposed to resolve problems and prevent recurrence. In the Governor's Office in Oregon, we came up with what remains 25 years later the simplest and most elemental answer:

> * A uniform tax on the potential energy content of all exhaustible energy sources at the point of extraction.

> * An extraction tax on the removal of all raw materials from natural storage.[1]

Income from such taxes can fund transition to more productive resource use as well as financing general governmental operation. Discouraging extraction of irreplaceable resources encourages use of renewable ones. *Improved economic performance resulting from such taxes is expected even if tax rates were as high as 10% of GDP.*[2]

In 1992, the World Resources Institute in Washington released a detailed "Green Fee" study which concluded a Factor 2 (50%) to Factor 5 (80%) net savings from every dollar of taxes shifted from "goods" to "bads."[3] Support for such ecological tax reform (ETR) is growing among economists seeing its potential for changing current perverse incentive structures, for reducing undesirable taxes, improving employment, and for environmental deregulation. The more that tax structures shift profitability from doing "bad" (pollution) to doing "good" (resource productivity), the more industry voluntarily aligns its practices without cumbersome regulation.

ETR has received support from the European Commission, British traffic planners, environmentalists, and the Business Council for Sustainable Development. Businesses relate to its potential for further deregulation and letting prices, rather than bureaucrats, tell the ecological truth. Engineers applaud the technological scope of the efficiency revolution. Scandinavian countries and the Netherlands have already implemented ETR CO_2/energy taxes. Germany, Belgium, and Austria have introduced green charges on certain products. The UK has implemented escalating gasoline and landfill taxes.[4]

Advertising

Centralized institutions and economic systems are neither efficient nor effective. They are a rarity in natural systems. What they do well is *centralize* profit and power into a few pockets. One of the largest incentives toward centralization is advertising. If we eliminate the centralizing power of advertising that adds $55 billion to the cost of our purchases, plus the resultant shipping of things back and forth and all the paper shuffling required to manage such large enterprises, what remains is what has been documented again and again. *Local production from local resources for local needs is usually considerably more efficient.*

Governmental policies can encourage or discourage unnecessary work. Advertising adds an average of 20% to the cost of many consumer goods. It doesn't add benefit to the product itself. The same can be said for the excessive transportation back and forth of materials in the process of centralized production of goods. Such activities are prime candidates for elimination by more resource-productive alternatives. Success of non-namebrand products and quality local "boutique-minibrands," such as microbrew beers, are showing the profitability of eliminating such costs. Eliminating tax write-offs of most advertising expenditures, and terminating preferential postage rates for bulk advertising mail can assist in the process. Changing financing of public airwave media such as radio and TV from advertising to public or view-financed, as in Europe; removing advertising from schools and busses; and other government actions can also assist.

Curitiba and Gaviotas[5]

It *is* possible to think outside of the box. With no outside funding, virtually no debt financing, and a population growth from 300,000 to 2,100,000 in 40 years, the Brazilian city of Curitiba has developed an integrative example of comprehensive, creative approaches to solving urban problems. Its unsubsidized bus-based public transit system using private operating firms is considered the world's finest. It has the capacity of a subway system, but cost 100 times less to build, and was constructed in four years. Adding new express lanes takes only six months. It carries (by choice) 75 percent of the city's commuters – 1.9 million passengers per weekday.

Flood control, wastewater, recycling, education, housing, parks, industrial development and health care have all been developed with the same community-based creative pragmatism. Novel partnerships between public, non-profit, community and private business have permitted new and successful solutions to problems. With dedication to solutions that are simple, fun, fast, and cheap, the city has created a major park in twenty days, a vast recycling program within months of its conception, and its first pedestrian mall in 48 hours.

Resources are used frugally, the scale of solutions matches those of the problems, and are tied together in a multi-dimensional, health-enhancing way. Value and service rewards are aligned to inspire and engage the entire community to achieve solutions that *everyone* benefits from. Its success is based on its values: respect for the citizen/owner of all public assets and services, both because all people deserve respect and because they will assume responsibility to help solve other problems if they feel respected. Creative approaches to all scales of public institutions can achieve dynamic success in solving persistent problems.

Gaviotas, in contrast, was built from scratch by a group of visionaries in the desolate rain-leached savannas of eastern Colombia. Beginning in 1971, they have developed a whole technology for the Third World, developed *by* the Third World – affordable, doable, maintainable, and which works. An automated irrigation system doesn't use computers – instead, a cylinder of expansive clay squeezes the water line shut when the soil is wet, and shrinks to let water flow when the soil is dry. Solar collectors that work in the rain. Solar kitchens, and "kettles" to sterilize drinking water. Windmills light enough to convert tropical breezes into energy. Ultra-efficient pumps to tap deep aquifers – easy enough to operate that they are hooked up to the children's seesaws.

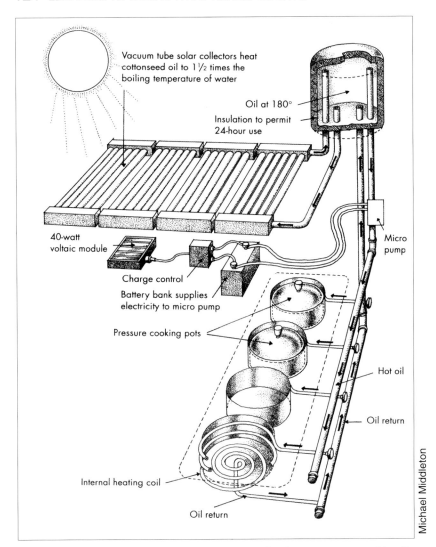

Vacuum tube solar collectors heat cottonseed oil to 1½ times the boiling temperature of water

Oil at 180°

Insulation to permit 24-hour use

40-watt voltaic module

Charge control

Battery bank supplies electricity to micro pump

Pressure cooking pots

Micro pump

Hot oil

Oil return

Internal heating coil

Oil return

Michael Middleton

Solar heating system for the hospital kitchen at Gaviotas uses vegetable oil rather than water, allowing high enough temperatures for cooking. Insulated storage tank allows 24-hour use of the stoves.

The aluminum-laden soil would only grow a harsh grass, but the researchers worked out hydroponic systems to grow food. Then they found a Caribbean pine tree that would grow in the soil, added micronutrients and mycorrhizal fungi, and began planting 2 million seedlings a year. In eight years, the trees were over fifty feet tall, producing wood and harvestable resin. And in the shelter of the trees, a diverse, indigenous tropical forest is regenerating, with dozens of species of wildlife.

The Gaviotans, now self-sufficient themselves in energy, have become a Columbian "Peace Corps," traveling throughout the country, given safe passage by warring factions, and leaving behind a trail of village wells, safe drinking water, solar collectors, and enhanced food-growing techniques. Starting fresh, with wholistic goals and approach to problems, they've shown the immense ability we have to solve seemingly intractable problems and create healthy, affordable, and rewarding lives for entire communities.

Both Curitiba and Gaviotas are living proof that inspired leadership can transform our lives and demonstrate that *every* context can be transformed by the new perspectives on economics.

Cradle To Grave Responsibility

As a result of governmental action pioneering the concept of "extended product responsibility", German (and now other European and Japanese) industries are designing everything from refrigerators to cars to office equipment for easy disassembly, repair, and recycling. This applies to industrial chemicals as well, resulting in the "rental" of chemical services, with the supplier taking back used chemicals for repurification and reuse. As a result, packaging recycling in Germany has jumped from 12 percent to 86% in five years. BMW's recyclable design of the Z-1 sports car had a bonus of making repairs easier. Labeling of thermoplastics has made possible their high-level recycling. Solvents are now recovered and reused over a hundred times. Dupont's Petretec process now *indefinitely* regenerates throw-away polyester film at the same quality but costing 25% less.[6]

Poverty

One political faction demands return to "family values," one-earner households, and reduced government expenditures and bureaucracies. Another faction demands increases in government programs and expanded employment to help the poor. Is there common ground in this and other political issues?

Repeated studies have shown that available jobs – *including government jobs* – pay considerably less than living wages. In Oregon, a "living wage" for a single adult in the year 2000 was $11/hour; while a "family wage" to support a family with two children was $18/hour. Forty percent of available jobs paid less than living wages for a single person, while 70% of available jobs paid less than "family wage" minimums. Sixty-five percent of *employed* minorities, sixty percent of women, and forty percent of all men earn *less* than a living wage. While living wages nationally are between $10/ and $20/hr, federal minimum wages are between $5.50 and $5.75/hour. The Oregon minimum is unusually high at $6.50/hour.[7] Clearly, in an economy dominated by large institutions, the individual job-seeker does not have leverage to obtain fair wages.

It would seem that raising minimum wages to "living wage" levels would provide multiple benefits. If *half* of the *workers* are below the poverty level, "living" wages would cause massive reduction in the need for government bureaucracy and poverty programs. It would seem that "family value" advocates should support raising them *even higher* – to "family wage" levels so that a single wage-earner could support a family.

If a state raised minimum wages, wouldn't it lose jobs to other states? Oregon hasn't. And if it did, the state would actually save paying significant costs of growth. (See Chapter Six) And is the loss of a below-poverty-level job something to mourn? With economic globalization, it is safe to assume that any jobs that are not tied to a location have *already* been exported to low-wage less-industrialized countries. So who is the government benefiting by not requiring the payment of living wages?

Paying taxes to support government activity to pay welfare-assistance to employed people because their employers don't pay a living wage, which they should be required to do to begin with, *does* seem crazy. This one doesn't even need numbers to figure out.

Transportation and Land-Use Zoning
In the automobile enthusiasm of the 1950's, communities established zoning requirements separating living and work, and requirement for parking spaces in commercial developments. We've learned since that automobile-centered development doubles the land required for many uses, and makes those very facilities inaccessible by public transit or foot, forcing the use of the automobile. Many European cities have subsequently banned automobiles from central areas during certain hours. Others have changed laws to eliminate parking requirements, tax the number of parking places provided, and require provision of transit passes to workers.

Car-sharing organizations (the equivalent of neighborhood car rental organizations) are expanding in many cities in the U.S. and Europe. Car-sharing in Berlin has cut member's car ownership by 75% and auto-commuting by 90%.[8] The role of rental automobiles in public

Neighborhood car rental in Kyoto, Japan. A shared facility allows availability of vehicles without having to add car storage space on each person's property.

transit is finally being addressed.[9] Cities like Kyoto, which require proof of a parking place for purchase of a car, are home to growing numbers of neighborhood car rental facilities. After a rigorous analysis, Portland, Oregon voted down construction of a Westside Bypass freeway in favor of new zoning for transit-oriented development where people live within walking distance of work, shopping and public transit.

These innovative shifts in dealing with transportation needs are a beautiful example of *cascading* benefits that increase as certain thresholds are reached. Car-sharing or neighborhood car rentals make a variety of vehicles available to everyone, reuse the vehicles for daytime business and evening personal use, avoid the land needed for automobile parking and storage, and reduce need for freeways for commuting. Mixed-use and transit-oriented development reduces *need* for auto use and freeways. With less use, shift to car-sharing reduces car ownership, making possible conversion of existing garages to apartments and micro-businesses, and driveways to gardens as building efficiency improve. This generates more people density for local shopping, neighborhood activities, etc. Less income is needed for transportation, less public infrastructure is required for utilities, and less pollution is generated.

Well-Being Indicators

What we see *should* be what we get. Statistics try to help us see how well we are doing. Increases in expenditures and incomes are lauded in current economic statistics as increasing well-being. Yet having to spend more on medical care can represent the cost of greater illness as easily as greater care and resultant health. Increases in income may reflect inflation, higher costs of living, or having to work two jobs to make ends meet.

There are also important things we don't pay attention to because we fail to measure them. And we see crime, drug and alcohol addiction, abuse, terrorist bombings, homelessness, and other "problems" as puzzling, costly, and unsolvable separate issues. Yet, as discussed earlier, in reality they are all symptoms of the *same* disease – a disease of the spirit arising from our ignoring the human, emotional, psychological and spiritual dimensions of our lives. Our statistics don't list "diseases of the spirit."

Our patterns of work, living, education – indeed all our base values and institutions – frequently prevent the healthy self-esteem, mutual respect, being of value, joy, happiness, grief and pain which are inherent dimensions of a healthy life. By taking rather than giving, by the overt and covert violence of our agriculture, medicine, forestry, business management, and personal relationships, we create immense hidden costs and damage to our lives. These are not, of course, reflected in the indicators we focus on of what our way of life *does* do successfully. But they show up as unanticipated and costly problems elsewhere that we have to pay to deal with. Dealing with their root causes can improve our quality of life as radically as reducing our cost of living.

Economics has relied in the past on simple "welfare indicators" such as *Gross National* (now called *"Domestic"*) *Product*, which basically measure industrial throughput. Producing a car that lasts twice as long would show up in the GDP as a major loss, when in reality it represents doubling the work productivity to provide transportation for the same number of years. Major things that don't show up in the GDP are work in the informal and home sector, and depletion of the resources left for future generations. Environmental degradation, and the costs of violence and inequity show up inversely as the work required to rectify the problems.

Alternative indicators, such as the *Genuine Progress Indicator* (GPI), also known as the *Index of Sustainable Economic Welfare* (ISEW),

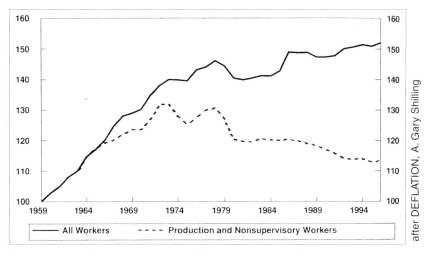

after DEFLATION, A. Gary Shilling

For most Americans, real compensation per hour, and other indicators of well-being have declined steadily since the 1970s, with quality of life impacted even more.

or the *Calvert/Henderson Quality-of-Life Indicators* do a far better job of measuring what contributes to quality of life.[10] Since the mid-1970s, the correlation between GDP and alternative indices has vanished, with most of the *apparent* growth shown on GDP reflecting remedial costs, and "bads" and nuisances being treated as if they were benefits to us. GPI or C-H QOL Indicators have more accurately reflected what most people feel . . .we are running harder to stay in the same place.

We tend to focus on things that show, and show positively, on the radar screen of statistics we are looking at. Governmental adoption of more accurate indicators can help us focus on things that bring real, and more direct, improvement in our quality of life.

TRUE SECURITY

What does fear cost? I warned, as early as 1982, that a wealthy and complex society like ours is very vulnerable to sabotage and terrorism.[11] We've since seen frightening confirmation of that vulnerability. A single bullet can (and has) shut down an entire electrical distribution grid, and accidentally burst the Alaska Pipeline, spilling 300,000 gallons of oil. A single handful of plutonium scattered from an office building window can threaten the lives of hundreds of thousands of people. One anti-tank rocket fired at an LNG storage tank can create another Hiroshima. The September 11, 2001, plane-bombing of the World Trade Center and the Pentagon, and subsequent anthrax mailings have made that vulnerability heart-wrenchingly apparent.

The history of such acts shows their variety, ease of execution, and virtual impossibility of prevention or retaliation. The September 11 events underline the importance of our voluntary and willing adjustment to new global conditions, values and aspirations. Regardless of how much overt military power we possess, terrorism will eventually escalate to a state of siege within the U.S. itself if our relations with other nations continue to deteriorate and if our denial of the sacred dimensions of life continues.

Combined with our curious assistance to nuclear proliferation, we could easily find ourselves either blown off the map or held hostage for a new economic and social world order. It is better that we initiate needed changes ourselves.

Inequity and poverty cause survival fears in the poor, and fears in the rich that the poor might take action to achieve equity. Wealth causes fear of theft, of loss, of inadequacy, of not being capable of getting by without wealth. Nuclear arms generate fear in everyone. Fear of job security causes timidity and loss of productivity and innovation. Inequitable access to resources causes immense military expenditures. The nightly news casts an ever-wider net to find stories of fear, accidents, disasters – and only rarely the good and wonderful things that give a sense of fullness in our lives.

Fear-related expenditures are not small – police and military costs, guns, gated-communities, security systems, all kinds of insurance, airport security, the medical costs of violence and other problems caused by fear, costs of restricting information, and the institutional costs which arise from fear. Listed and unlisted military costs already constitute more than 30% of federal governmental expenditures. *Reducing what leads to fear is more productive and far less costly than paying what results from it.*

If we eliminate poverty by creating an equitable society, we eliminate the need for governmental poverty programs. If we make an order of magnitude reduction in our demands for resources, and help the rest of the world to do the same, we dramatically reduce the need to fight over resources, or pay to send troops to the Persian Gulf. Economic equity also eliminates much of the desperation, fear and anger giving rise to crime. Restoration of self-esteem, mutual respect, and being of value to our communities heals the diseases of the spirit that lay behind our drug and alcohol addiction, spouse and child abuse. These are some of the interconnected secondary benefits of these actions.

Two-thirds of our prisons are filled from minor drug-related offenses. Prohibition, however, hasn't worked any better for marijuana than for alcohol. (Every society seems to need some means of taking a break from everyday reality.) Separating the disease of addiction from the crimes of trafficking heavy drugs, taking the profit out of drug sales, and eliminating the economic and emotional poverty that underlies addiction can accomplish more for our health and security than our massive expenditures on jails, drug enforcement and crime programs. Our prison population is nearly six times greater than 25 years ago, though crime rates have fallen. Our expenditures are higher now for prisons than for schools.

When we add up the economic costs of fear – let alone the emotional costs – the alternative of reducing the causes of fear becomes a bargain. Less demand for resources, greater equity, and a larger proportion of our resources going towards creating real health and well-being go a long way towards reducing the costs of dealing with what happens in their absence.

It is important that we fully understand our changing role in the world; realize the gross injustices that lie behind our past patterns of interaction with others; and put our efforts into helping rather than hindering the transition to more equitable, fair, and humane international relationships. We would be better off in the future with at least a small legacy of understanding, respect, and helpfulness rather than bitterness, obstructionism and hatred. Our future security lies more in the goodwill of others than in tending to our own narrow self-interest.[12]

True security requires that *all* parties feel secure. Economic and financial self-reliance and equity of power are essential, but beyond these factors a much more important dimension of security lies in the willingness to help others in time of need. That willingness comes from common beliefs and as reciprocity – repayment for past aid and helpfulness. We will have real security only when we base our interactions on such reciprocity as well as on friendship, respect, admiration and love. Building that kind of security will require a vastly different attitude and approach than we have followed.[13]

TOTAL COSTS AND PUBLIC POLICY

In 1994 I was asked by students at the University of Oregon for help. The University administration was planning to tear down the 50-year old married student apartments (surplus WW-II military housing) and replace them with new structures. On the surface that sounded like a good idea. But many students, feeling there was nothing wrong with the existing complex other than deferred maintenance, saw no reason to tear down what they saw as perfectly good buildings. And they feared, rightly, that rental costs would increase dramatically.

The University commissioned a study which said it would be cheaper to replace the buildings than repair them. The students didn't believe the report – it went against "tummy" logic. So they asked me to review it.[14]

My conclusions were remarkably different, and interesting in what they revealed the University was leaving out of their comparisons. I found that the lifecycle cost of new construction would be approximately 60% *more* than maintaining the existing buildings. And looking at the *total project* costs, the "new" option would be approximately 3.5 times greater than that of the existing buildings. This represented a difference of over $111,000/unit over a 50 year period. With a 60% larger size of the proposed replacement units factored in, the disparity in costs was even greater ($194,634/unit). And including taxpayer bond subsidies, *the new units would cost 4.7 times as much as the "extended-life" existing units.* The students had reason to be concerned about an almost 5-fold potential increase in costs.

This was a Factor-5 cost difference (almost 80% savings) which involved only better perceptions of the true costs of alternatives. It involved no technological innovations, no new anything . . . just simple math with intention to see what true costs were involved. (Significant and equivalent energy and durability savings could additionally be achieved with either option. But again, with the maintenance" option, they could be achieved on a "pay-as-you-go" basis.)

Why the differences between the University study and mine?

* The University study didn't credit *the economic and financial value of the existing structures*, or to allow for component life cycles which in many cases realistically can exceed 50 years.

Relocated Amazon Married Student Housing buildings continue to provide very low-cost housing for people in the community. Nothing fancy, but adequate and affordable.

* *Debt service* was ignored in cost comparisons. This practice of focusing on "construction" costs rather than *total* project costs misrepresented true project costs, as debt service is a real cost of options that require it, and usually by far the largest single cost of a project. A crucial factor in comparison between replacement and maintenance of existing buildings was that work on the "maintenance" option could be done on a "pay-as-you-go" basis, *without* financing, while new construction *required* major financing.

* In addition to actual construction costs, *total project costs* also include site and development (similar here); "soft" costs such as design fees, financing, administrative costs, furnishings and appliances, sales charges (not applicable here), etc. Maintenance of existing buildings did not require hiring architects and engineers, in itself representing a 10% additional cost beyond the construction costs of the buildings.

* The University study compared costs of identical sized units, but *the actual new units proposed were 60% larger,* with commensurate higher costs.

* *"Tax-free" bonds* were proposed for financing the new structures. In addition to the face value debt service, every dollar of such bonds issued represent a cost to the citizens of the state of replacing taxes avoided by the purchasers of the bonds.

* Even if the *financial* costs were the same for extended life vs. replacement of the Amazon Housing, the *economic costs would still be considerably different.* Existing investment in site development, foundations, structural framing, insulation, and other elements of the building with long life cycles would not be abandoned or need replacement in the "maintenance" option. No trees would be cut for framing lumber or siding, as would be necessary in the "new" option. Electric boxes and wiring, interior walls and ceilings, etc. would not be thrown away and require resources to replace, nor the landfill impacts of the demolition of the existing buildings incurred. The financial costs of the "maintain" option also represented a greater ratio of employment to resource use, a strong argument in its favor when viewed from the standpoint of sustainable economics.

My review of the University study brought to the surface the tendency we all have to ignore or exclude costs with might be prejudicial to the decisions we want made, and our lack of experience in trying to visualize and include the total costs of our actions. The Amazon Family Housing provided a unique opportunity to demonstrate the significant savings inherent in making what we have serve us longer and better. In the final resolution of the project, the students were successful in having a portion of the structures saved and moved to another site. They continue to provide low-cost housing to the community.

This was a particularly interesting study in the immense savings it found available just by rethinking conventional economic decision-making. It is especially applicable to other public policy decisions and reviewing institutional costs and structures. An approach developed initially to seek major reduction in energy use was found generally applicable to much broader realms of economics.

AUTOMATE THE RICH, NOT THE POOR[15]

Almost daily we're faced with new examples of automation wiping out whole categories of jobs and putting people out of work by the tens and hundreds of thousands. In the last twenty years, automation moved of the production line: electronic grocery check-outs eliminated 100,000 jobs in check-out, inventory control and product pricing. Automation of banking procedures – both electronic tellers and automated posting – eliminated similar numbers of jobs. Telephone operators, newspaper typesetters clerical work in businesses, and field-work in produce growing have all felt the ominous weight of job elimination. We're expected to accept the wrenching impacts of these changes as the inevitable side-effects of more efficient business methods from which we supposedly all benefit.

That might be an acceptable trade-off if jobs were not the only means presently of sharing our nation's wealth, if it were not just low-income jobs that are affected, and if automation had not eliminated so many jobs that it is very difficult for many people to find another job. The truth is that the goal of most automation is change in distribution of wealth and power. Machines don't strike, computers don't ask for raises or a fair proportion of the profit from their work, and automated assembly lines don't talk back to the foreman, get sick, or get tired.

There is, however, another kind of automation we've ignored – one that has very different social impacts. *Automate the _rich_ instead of the poor.* It's a people-oriented automation which increases equity and gives benefits directly to the less wealthy. Automating the rich by applying Factor Ten economics to professional services can eliminate at least as much unnecessary work and save at least as much money as automating the poor. It can help obtain a more equitable balance of power and wealth in our society. It requires displacement of fewer people to obtain the same savings, and the displaced people have more skills and ability to find other jobs.

Most every well-paid trade or profession has gotten that way because they can perform highly valuable services. "Automating" those services is not an attempt to eliminate or underpay such services, but to free people from *unnecessary* need for those services. At the same time it can free the professionals and tradespeople from wasting their time with unneeded or routine work so they can be freer to deal with the more challenging work. Lawyers aren't needed for every divorce, doctors for every sore throat, or plumbers for every leaky faucet. They're great to have when really needed, but being forced to use them when not needed does nobody good.

Interestingly enough, some of the rich have already automated themselves, but haven't told anyone, so are still coming around to collect their ample paychecks. A good example is the real estate business. Most homes are sold through realtors, who collect an average of 6% of the sales price on every house they sell. That's $6,000 on a $100,000 house. And houses are bought and sold on an average of every 8 years. In a thirty year period, that means that many people end up paying realtors a total of at least $22,500 in commissions. That same $22,500 – if used to reduce the mortgage carried on the houses – would result in a savings over the same period of $50-60,000!

The necessary work done by realtors varies, in part with buyers' individual needs. But a change has occurred in the real estate business that can eliminate much unnecessary realty work. In most communities, realtors have set up Multiple Listing Services. A MLS allows a realtor to show a buyer any house listed with any realtor in the community. The commission is split between the listing agent and the selling agent. One interesting result is that the person selling the house ends up paying a realtor to help the buyer purchase the house for less.

The mechanics and possibilities of the system itself are even more interesting. The seller fills out a card with detailed information such as lot size, number and size of rooms, kind of heating, tax assessment, mortgage situation, and amount of insulation. The realtor sends the card, along with a picture of the house to the MLS, which puts out a weekly computer-prepared booklet or internet site containing the pictures and information on all the houses for sale in the community, broken down by location, price bracket, number of bedrooms, etc.

The catch is that the MLS doesn't cost anywhere near $6,000 per house listed. In fact, a normal charge to realtors is $100/month for the service, plus $50 charge for each listing sold. In comparison, the cost you end up eventually paying is *one thousand times as much*. A MLS operated as a non-profit, community-owned *Community Housing Exchange* could give such listing information to prospective buyers, have them available electronically on the Internet, and in libraries and neighborhood centers, employment services, personnel offices of businesses, shopping centers and banks.

Simple guidebooks for homebuyers and sellers can explain what to look for, how not to get taken, and how to make a fair deal. People could still go to realtors for special assistance wanted. Such Community Housing Exchanges are an example of a kind of automation that would save the average family far more than automated grocery check-outs, would reduce need for a well-paid service, would lessen rather than contribute to inequalities of wealth and power, and could be accomplished through public action.

Automating the rich often doesn't even need the expensive equipment needed to replace the poor. Although some lucrative jobs can probably be automated in this way, automation is probably over-kill for many high-dollar occupations. Competition might be equally successful. We are forced to employ and pay for many services only because monopolies have successfully been set up through legislation forbidding practice of law, plumbing, medicine, architecture, etc. without a license, or have limited entry into the field by controlling apprenticeship programs or educational requirements. In such cases, the simple technology of the ballot box can reduce unnecessary jobs or excessive charges without a need for any more sophisticated kinds of "automation." Here are some candidates:

Lawyers are made virtually necessary for many of the rituals of life because of the labyrinthine wording and procedures that have evolved (largely with their help) on public documents. But some states have worked out standard forms and sample fill-in paragraphs for different situations which make incorporation of a small business a simple $10 procedure. Standard rental and sales contracts for housing have been developed by public assistance groups that are fair to all parties instead of putting all the eggs in the landlord's basket. Do-it-yourself divorce manuals now make it possible to eliminate the need for lawyers in most divorces.

The State of Pennsylvania has put out a *Consumer's Guide to Personal Bankruptcy*, and do-it-yourself bankruptcy guides are available. Many small-claims courts will not allow lawyers to represent *either* party. These examples suggest that some of the need for big dollar, big language go-betweens can be eliminated.

Undertakers are another expensive service that is beginning to be "automated." Co-operative burial associations have made dignified low-cost burial and memorial services available. Even some commercial undertakers, feeling the pressure, now make available a simple $250 cremation if you succeed in escaping their play on your emotions for a multi-thousand-dollar extravaganza.

Bankers are being devalued through broadening the permissible activities of credit unions where people can control and profit themselves from the use of their money. Public no-interest revolving loan programs for housing can "automate" some very expensive "banker's business" in the mortgage department.

Plumbers are an example of trades who restrict entry to keep wages high, and have a triple tier of people we have to pay . . . the person doing the work, the person who has the plumber's license, and the inspector who sees if they've done it wrong anyhow. "Automating" here means merely removing restrictions on who does the work – if an inspector is necessary, that is all the control that should be needed.

Administrators are the highest paid jobs in almost any organization, and they seem to pile up in pyramids whenever an organization becomes more centralized. Since they set the pay scales themselves, they are certain they're worth the most. Automating them requires tumbling down the pyramid of centralization – setting up autonomous, locally-controlled, small-scale organizations that don't require such bureaucratic skills.

Educators are an example of an occupation that affects us by wasting years of our lives as well as by consuming great amounts of public and personal funds. Educational requirements for many occupations have almost no correlation to a person's ability to do the job – they're just a legalized means to force people to support educational institutions and collect unnecessary "certificates." Many occupations have collaborated in this requirement for irrelevant educational degrees merely to gain status or to justify higher wages.

A number of professions require both graduation from a certified academic program and passing a licensing examination, or heavily penalize people with work experience rather than academic experience that want to take the exam. Architects, lawyers, registered nurses, CPAs, beauty parlor operators, realtors, and even massage workers require passing this double academic and qualifying examinations. Some states are beginning to eliminate such educational requirements for public jobs, relying on what you have done rather than what you've been "taught." Academic training requirements should be eliminated in state licensing requirements where duplicated by a licensing examination.

The concept of automation needs to be taken out of the hourly-wage-earner's world, turned on its head, and applied to the top end of our income pyramid. It mostly means relearning that we are competent to do things ourselves that we've been taught require specialized, expensive skills of other "professionals." It requires a sense of social justice necessary to question the status-quo in "professional" occupations. And it requires putting together simple alternatives that can serve significant proportions of our needs. If automation, or elimination of unnecessary jobs, or reducing unnecessary costs is valuable at all, then it's even more valuable applied to the high-paid jobs of the rich.

---

[1] "Cosmic Economics," Joel Schatz and Tom Bender, OERP, 1974.

[2] FACTOR FOUR, above.

[3] *"Green Fees,"* Bob Repetto & Roger Dower, World Resources Institute, 1992. See also Charles Ballard and Steven Medema's *"The Marginal Efficiency Effect of Taxes and Subsidies..."*, Michigan State University, 1992. and *"Tax Waste, Not Work,"* Redefining Progress, 1992.

[4] See FACTOR FOUR, above, for more detailed discussion of ETR.

[5] For Curitiba, see *"Curitiba"*, Chap. 2 in HOPE, HUMAN AND WILD, Bill McKibben, Little, Brown, 1995; and Chap 14 in NATURAL CAPITALISM, Hawken and Lovins, Little, Brown, 1999. For Gaviotas, see GAVIOTAS, Alan Weisman, Chelsea Green, 1998.

[6] For dozens of examples, see FACTOR FOUR and NATURAL CAPITALISM, above.

[7] DAILY ASTORIAN, June 22, 2001.

[8] See "Car Sharing in Berlin," Von Weizsächer and Lovins, FACTOR FOUR, Earthscan, 1997.

[9] See *"Rent-Alls,"* Tom Bender, AORTA Bulletin, Jan 1995. Reprinted in IN CONTEXT, Issue 44, July 1996.

[10] For ISEW, see Clifford Cobb's appendix to FOR THE COMMON GOOD, Herman Daly and John Cobb, Beacon Press, 1989. For C/H-QOL, see Hazel Henderson, PARADIGMS OF PROGRESS, Knowledge Systems, 1991. Also, FACTOR FOUR, above.

[11] *"True Security"*, RAIN Magazine, Oct. 1982; also "The End of Nuclear War", 1986. This prescient article graphically showed modern industrial society's extreme vulnerability to terrorism. *Foreign Affairs* rejected it as "too theoretical." After September 11, 2001, few would think so. Also, BRITTLE POWER: Energy Strategy for National Security, Amory and L. Hunter Lovins, Brick House, 1982; SECURITY WITHOUT WAR, Hal Harvey and Mike Shuman, Westview, 1993.

[12] "Seek Wisdom, Not Vengeance," Tom Bender, Guest Column, DAILY ASTORIAN, Sept. 21, 2001; "Ten Easy Pieces of a Better World," Tom Bender, Guest Column, DAILY ASTORIAN, Oct. 31, 2001; ENDLESS ENEMIES: The Making of an Unfriendly World, Jonathan Kwitney, 1986.

[13] "Neighborhood Bully," Derrick Jensen, THE SUN, August, 2001.

[14] *"Amazon Student Family Housing,"* Tom Bender. April, 1994.

[15] *"Automate the Rich, Not the Poor,"* Tom Bender, RAIN Magazine, 1980.

Chapter 9
Economics Where People DO Matter

The differences between conventional economics and an economics of wholeness are more than the order-of-magnitude quantitative ones of human, material, and energy resource productivity. The most significant differences, as we're seeing, are *qualitative*. The different patterns and paths to our goals which yield immense productivity gains also transform our lives in other more basic ways. This chapter will try to give a sense of some of those differences.

WORK AND LEISURE

The *primary* products of work are not external. In reality, we work largely in order to change ourselves. It is *we* that want to be warmer, drier, or happier, and we work either to produce those changes directly or to indirectly make them possible. When the process of working to provide or purchase food or shelter can at the same time contribute directly to our happiness and well-being, why choose work patterns that destroy skills, self-respect, security, health, and happiness?

Productive work not only brings forth directly the goods and services needed for a comfortable existence, but also allows us to employ simultaneously our physical and mental processes to interact with the world around us. Such work brings us in touch with the integrity of the world, calling forth similar nature within us. It is a means to discover within the nature of our actions the nature of our selves, allowing us to bring our actions and internal rhythms into line with what we wish to be. It allows us to create, and to discover our abilities. It brings us into contact with others, and opens us to being changed by the nature and action of the world around us.

As well as a unity between the external and internal products of work, there is an essential unity between work and leisure that is important to our lives. Good work requires time for patience, thoroughness, and quality – time to explore untried possibilities and to refine and improve familiar ones. It requires focussed attention and peace of mind – free from distractions, pressures, and anxieties. It permits us to grow through it and to gain satisfaction from it. In short, *leisure is necessary for good work.* Similarly, leisure requires opportunity to do rewarding things, to avoid the boredom, restlessness, and lack of meaning that we associate with "free time."

Quantity of work – either in number of hours spent "working", or in amount of "output" – is not an effective measure of either the inner or outer value of work. Our complex patterns of production and thoughtless decisions of what to produce result in efficient production of unimportant thing. *We spend, on an average, only about five hours a <u>week</u> in productive work.*[1] Better purpose in our work is more important than better efficiency. Making one good car rather than many junkers, one important scientific discovery rather than many trivial ones, or writing one good song rather than many ordinary ones, has greater lasting effect and value. The *quality* of what we produce is no less important than the *quantity.*

So much of our work is related to trivial purposes, to dealing with the logistics of unnecessary institutionalization, scale, and quantification, and to secondary purposes like gaining a promotion or becoming famous or infamous, that we lose sight of what meaningful, productive work is. Stress-related diseases have become one of our society's greatest problems, but we fail to connect that with the fact that our work patterns are riddled with stress, anxiety and tension. As a result, we forget to deal with the basic considerations of security of work and income and the freedom of pace, purpose, and process necessary for peace of mind and good work. We have so removed the rewards from work by how we approach and organize it that we only think of completing it and being free to seek reward in other activities. We have become, as Alan Watts might say, like singers whose only concern is to get to the end of the song most quickly. We have lost sight that joy is in the singing itself.

For each of us, changing our ways of work so that our entire lives become a continuous process of absorbing and rewarding action is likely to be different. But those outer changes all evolve out of similar changes in our attitudes. An important first step is probably to reduce our wants, and thus the work-produced income we demand – to give us more elbow room to evolve secure and rewarding work patterns, to free our time from distracting consumption patterns, and to learn to find satisfaction in the work itself rather than what it might ultimately provide.

Secondly, we need to realize that we can never accomplish all that we dream of – that dreams expand equally with accomplishment – and that we should look to what we are doing, and doing it well, for reward rather than to what we might do someday in the future. Someone else will eventually accomplish, get done, or discover what we don't, and no matter what we *do* achieve, it will end in dust. There should be no guilt in doing something thoroughly and finding reward in doing it well. The alternative results in racing from one thing to another, and leaving each half- and poorly-done and ourselves in a dither from our haste.

Knowing that we can never finish all of what we dream, we find the peace to explore the limitless perfections and possibilities that lie in each thing we do. We understand and rejoice in the extravagance of nature that produces the perfect wonder of hummingbirds and wildflowers and snowflakes and waves breaking on a beach, and put the same wonder into all that we do. Knowing that we can't do all, we develop a bulls-eye intuition to sense where our effort will have most effect and give the greatest rewards. Our whole sense of accomplishment becomes transformed.

Mindlessness is not necessarily bad. We tend to try to avoid such repetitive work, seeking to get for ourselves the parts of work that are exciting and creative and require our fullest attention, while trying to pass on to someone else the routine parts of a job. They both, however, are important and necessary to us. If properly approached, the mindless parts of work provide us a wonderful opportunity to draw upon our unconscious and intuitive dimensions – in melding our hands and minds into one seamless flow. Whether typing or washing dishes or laying bricks, "mindless" working rests our conscious processes, opens our receptivity, allows problems to stew and work in our unconscious, and simultaneously restores and strengthens the unity of our selves with our actions that conscious processes destroy.

True leisure requires us to be at peace and at rest with ourselves and our world. So does good work. It involves a deep acceptance and love of all parts of life, and brings a particular relaxedness, freshness, and readiness to work which cannot be confused with the tense activity of our more familiar way of doing things. Leisure is a mental and spiritual attitude, not merely the existence of time left over after work. It means not pushing things but letting them happen, and being *open* and connected in the process. It is, as Joseph Pieper says, a receptive attitude of mind – not only the occasion but also the *capacity* for steeping oneself in the whole of Creation. Work performed from leisure is renewing and revitalizing. It touches and draws upon life-giving powers, and opens a path of effortless action that lies far beyond the conditions of work that we have set for ourselves today.[2]

Heinrich Kley

❖

LET FANTASIES BE FANTASIES

Advertising is a highly refined exploitation of something we do all the time – creating fantasies and then attempting to fulfill them. Maybe it's a fantasy about having a new car, or being famous, or making love to a certain person – it doesn't matter. What we rarely notice about such fantasies is that they never stop coming. We put a lot of effort into fulfilling one and scarcely catch our breath before another one arises to take its place . . . a little bit better stereo, a little bit bigger house, a little more luxurious car, a little bit more glamorous lover.

No one ever tells us, and we rarely seem to see ourselves, that *having fantasies is what the whole thing is about* – not destroying them by making them "real." What if, instead of knocking ourselves out fulfilling fantasy after fantasy, we just kept a few unfulfilled dreams? Think of all the energy we would save inventing new dreams as well as realizing old ones. Just *dream* about that mansion or that job – and savor the dream. The dream is likely at least as good as the reality anyhow! Dreams don't leak, get sick, or need repairs.

If we can thus separate our fantasies from our needs, and just let them be that, we can live comfortable, relaxed and rewarding lives with a fraction of the effort we spend chasing after our own desire to have things to dream about.[3]

JOBS, HUMBUG!

A look at jobs can give a sense of the different rewards inherent in a soft economics path. Efforts to stem industrial pollution, prevent clear-cutting of wilderness areas, lower military expenditures, or stop unwise energy developments have widely been countered by claims that they would put people out of work. Careful analysis has shown, of course, that quite the opposite to be true – capital-intensive automation is the primary cause of unemployment. *Any* expenditure of money will provide some jobs. Military activities and energy production actually provide few jobs, however, while energy efficiency, pollution control, high-grade material recycling, and other resourceful technologies generate much more employment per dollar than do their conventional alternatives.

But the job question goes deeper than that. Work is the only mechanism in our existing economic system that gives people access to the wealth produced by our society, and job-intensive processes are viable means of escaping the capital- and energy-intensive processes we can no longer afford. But jobs that are derived from the unnecessary production of goods and services, or the use unnecessarily laborious means of production are a waste of human energy. A throw-away society that discards, wastes, and demeans the human work that goes into producing throw-aways is crazier still. If there isn't enough necessary work to employ all of us forty hours a week, then it seems more important that we should each work less rather than causing unemployment. We should develop a system of income distribution based on more than just paid work.

Unemployment is a measure of inequitable access to work. If we can provide for our needs with half the work, then we *each* should have to work only half as much, not create unemployment for some while others work more.

As important as who works and how much should be done is the effect of work on the worker. E. F. Schumacher has pointed out that modern technology has taken over the work of human hands to the degree that only 3-1/2% of our time is spent in actual productive work. The rest of the time is spent in non-productive paper shuffling, eating, sleeping, watching television or just killing time. It has multiplied the amount of non-productive work that would not be necessary if our technology were less "modern." And it has taken most of the normal human satisfaction out of the real productive work. Work can and should produce changes in the worker as well as to the materials being worked. Skills, self-respect, self-confidence, a sense of contributing value to the community, and a deepening understanding of those things that make up our world are destroyed today, rather than developed by our system of work and production.

If we focus on something other than increasing machine displacement of human work, we can see remarkable new potentials. If, as Schumacher suggests, we *increased* our time spent in productive work *sixfold* – to all of 20% of our time, we would only need 1/6 of present productivity to produce as much as we do now. We would have six times as much time to do a *really* good job, to work leisurely and enjoy ourselves, to produce real quality and even beauty.

Jobs give us more than a paycheck. They give us a lot of satisfactions or dissatisfactions, security or ulcers. They lock us into a cash economy where we have little control over what we are paid for our work or what we pay for goods and services. They push us into specialization and dependence on others to take care of our needs. They usually tie us into a 40-hour week and a strongly hierarchical structure in which creative energy is diverted into taking advantage of others and resisting being taken advantage of. They split us into opposing and self-serving roles – producer and consumer, employer and employee, management and labor. Jobs, like store-bought bread, rarely come in different-sized slices – it's either full-time or no-time.

"A job" usually means working for someone else. Thought of "providing jobs" to counter unemployment usually ends up considering only those who can "provide" jobs – large institutions – rather than the less centralized and less manipulatable alternative of people creating work for themselves. Having a job is only *one* way of having work, and possibly the least likely way to have rewarding work. Having *jobs* may be as much a basic *cause* of social and economic problems as a solution to them.

Looking more broadly at work rather than just at jobs, we find that alternatives to our present job-centered economy provide radically different social benefits as well as rewards to the workers:

> * We can work for ourselves (self-employment).
> * We can provide for our own needs (self-reliance).
> * Or we can restrain our desires and work less (self-restraint).

It's amazing how much energy in a job goes into taking advantage of others or resisting being taken advantage of. Figuring out how to pay people less, or get more work out of them. Figuring out how to stretch coffee breaks and lunch, get to work late, get more sick days, to look like you're busy. Bucking for promotion. Taking credit for the work of people below you to get a raise. Passing on blame. Being angry at management for its stupidity or meanness. Unionizing to fight for fair wages and working conditions. Hassling with the *union* management. Hassling with corporate, union, and *government* demands. Feeling, rightly, that you probably don't matter.

Alternatives to jobs free us from huge amounts of this bad personal energy by avoiding the division of work into such conflicting and exploitive elements that are inherent in most present job relationships:

> * *Self-employment* avoids the division of interest between worker and management. You've no one to get mad at but yourself, there's no profit in trying to pull one over on yourself, and no ill feelings if you do so.

> * *Self-reliance* goes even further, by eliminating the split between the producer and consumer. You know what you're getting, and the price is right, because the price is whether you're willing to put in the necessary work to do it! We can fix our own cars, bake our own bread, make our own clothes, gather our own firewood, build our own homes or teach our own children, exactly as we want. No risk of us overcharging or cheating ourselves, no one to get mad at for sloppy work, no doubt as to the contents of our food or schooling. We can make things as simply or elaborately as we wish. We can work into the night or go fishing during banking hours.

* *Self-restraint* – reducing our "needs" – takes us another step towards surmounting divisive conflicts of interest. Demanding less reduces the amount of work that has to be done and thus our demands on our resources and each other. Every vacation trip or new car or new coat or fancy dinner or television set we decide we don't need is one less that has to be made, and one less we have to work to pay for.

The "job" relationship that is so common in industrial society puts us into a real double-bind. We're supposed to be efficient, productive, and work for the interests of our employer from 8 to 5. Then we abruptly turn around to be profligate consumers, buying for whim, vanity, luxury and prestige. At the same time we are trapped into an effective divide and conquer strategy by commercial interests. By dividing us alternately between working and consuming roles – neither of which we control or in which we can bargain as equal partners, we get milked coming and going.

As individual *consumers*, we have little power to ensure true quality or value in what we purchase. As individual *employees*, we have little power to gain fair working conditions or a fair division of income between our work and the inputs of management. As consumers or employees banded together into groups or unions with enough power to balance the corporations, we suddenly find ourselves with another large and powerful bureaucracy to deal with.

Ways of meeting our needs more directly and more simply may also meet them more satisfyingly. Self-confidence grows with self-reliance. The more we're responsible for satisfying our own needs, the less we're trapped in the frustrations, anger, and distrust that fill the marketplace and the workplace. Self-reliance minimizes a person's cash income and therefore taxes. Real needs can often be better known and more effectively met by the person having those needs.[4]

❖

LIFE WITHOUT FEAR

It is curious the degree to which, in a world of apparent material plenty, life is filled with fear. Fear of abuse, mugging, rape, murder. Fear of job loss, age, death. Fear of auto accidents, plane crashes, hurricanes, floods. Fear of inadequacy, failure, nuclear war, crippling disease. Fear of what the future may, or may not, hold.

In a community where we each care about, honor, and ensure the well-being of all life; where life is based on equity rather than greed, where we don't have to hide our fears and struggle alone, life gains a security and freedom unknown in a society of greed and growth. When the primary causes of violence and the reasons to fear others are minimized and violence itself not valued as a base belief of society, positive relations are possible. Where we identify with the well-being of all creation, the larger climatic, geologic, and evolutionary patterns of nature are seen and honored from within a different understanding. True security comes from equitable access to non-depleting resources, a stable supporting eco-system, and a real community to support and back our needs and ensure the emotional health of all.

The life-nurturing values and principles upon which sustainable communities are based result in freedom from some of the most emotionally-crippling dimensions of a society based on greed and growth.[5]

AN ECONOMY OF *GIVING*, NOT *TAKING*

An economics of wholeness is an economics of *giving*, not of *taking*. Giving is an integral part of loving, and loving is the root of holding things sacred essential to sustainability. It enriches the giver and the receiver both, and creates multiple value out of each and every exchange. If "What can I *give* in this situation?" is in our hearts every time we talk with or do something with someone, we not only leave a legacy of gifts in addition to our intended interaction, but we generate an enduring climate of trust, mutual caring, thankfulness and happiness which moves outward like the waves in the sea.[6]

A *giving* economy allows us opportunity to share the bounty we enjoy. It provides means to express thanks for other gifts received, and to give someone, some thing, or some place what we feel they deserve. It acknowledges that whenever any of us puts creativity into our lives we are creating something new which did not exist before, and making a gift of that to others. Enriching all, a *giving* economy stands in clear contrast to most exchanges today which often leaves the equally unhealthy feeling of having "put one over," or wonder if we've "been taken."

The gift economy of a community based on love and honoring gives multiple benefits, and fulfills our emotional as well as material needs, while providing the glue of love and trust essential to any enduring relationship.

LIVING FROM THE HEART

Excess material wealth and numbers, inequity, and unconcern for the rest of life poison our souls. *Taking from* rather than *caring for* others closes off our hearts. Closing ourselves off from the pain that we cause loses us the connectedness that gives life meaning. It sentences us to a life of psychological and emotional barrenness and meaningless existence. The only thing that can alleviate this pain is love, and opening ourselves to the vulnerability and pain of allowing love even in the face of our unloving behavior.[7]

A world where everyone wears masks, hides their feelings, and closes off connection with what lies outside their skin leads quickly to collective insanity. We grow up thinking we're weird because we're not happy – when all we are seeing is the masks that hide the feelings of inadequacy, unhappiness, anger and confusion of others. We close ourselves off from the flow of energy that generates, pervades and nurtures all life, with resulting illness and atrophy of our own lives.

As mentioned earlier, in truth we *can't* lie. Our unconscious interconnectedness knows the difference between what comes from the heart and what comes from the head. In the absence of living from the heart, we mistake our own masks and those of others for the underlying reality.

The actions necessary to move from a world of greed and violence to one of generosity and giving are simple and can be initiated by any of us. Speak from the heart. Let down our masks. Be willing to be vulnerable, and open our hearts to others. Honor and hold sacred all life. Deal with the roots of our fears. Learn to give. Seek wisdom and joy, not power.

These changes involve humility, trust, and vulnerability; facing and dealing with pain and its causes; dealing directly with hard questions of equity and fairness; and a 180^0 shift in the goals and operation of every aspect of our society. This sounds daunting, until we begin to understand and personally experience the deep personal and social rewards of those changes and the vast improvement in effectiveness inherent in them.

When we speak from the heart, we always speak the truth – our truth. It may not be a universal truth, but it is a real truth grown out of the unique life and experience of each of us. I can take your truth and add it to mine, and find a greater one. Your fear of losing a job if we cut back on over-logging or wasteful oil use is as real as my fear of a bigger collapse if we don't. In the open, we can take each of these truths and bring them together into a more encompassing one. And the acknowledgment of our individual realities can make it possible to work together to find solutions that encompass both.

Speaking from the heart, we can touch real issues, fight real demons, and make real progress. We can achieve true consensus and group support for all actions. With that, we lose all patience with the invisible walls created by our conventional patterns and rituals of conferences and meetings and confrontations which prevent real progress.

Living from the heart is the essence of true connection needed for sustainable and effective interpersonal relationships. It yields both the opportunity for others to understand and give to us, and for us to find right action in our interaction with others. It helps us gain the true rewards of self-esteem, mutual respect, and being of value to the community for our efforts – not just the material substitutes we settle for today.

SACRED SURROUNDINGS

Living in a sacred way transforms our surroundings as well as our lives. Not promoting consumption removes advertising from blue jeans and busses and billboards and the public eye. Living from the heart transforms our cities into ones which reflect passions, not inner poverty. Stabilizing our population and learning to give can transform our communities physically. Putting our effort into *better*, rather than *more*, our cities can, like cities such as Prague, come to reflect the pouring a thousand years of love into the places we live.[8]

Learning to honor all of Creation gives all of Creation an honored place in our surroundings - trees for *trees*, not trees for shade or cooling or recreation parks. Like the hill towns of Spain, the mountain villages of Austria, or the countryside of India, shrines and places of silence give ways to express thanks, to connect deeply with the rest of Creation, to honor the special power and energy of a place, and for our surroundings to express the sacredness with which we hold them.

Such communities find new ways to express a new unfolding of our understanding of the wonders of the universe and our place in it. These new reflections of our understanding are inevitably different from, yet capable of the same power as French gothic cathedrals, Japanese Zen gardens, Angkor Wat, or Persian mosques.

Sustainability requires that we learn to make where we *are* paradise, rather than to seek it through endless travel. In the process, we discover the special soul of each place and the ways to build and live in harmony with it; with ecological sensitivity, natural energy flows and native materials. Replacing tourism with pilgrimage transforms our energy in visiting and sharing places other than our own.[9]

These changes bring an unprecedented depth and richness of meaning to our surroundings and how they interact with our lives. Places have souls, and can connect with and enrich our own.

Living in a sacred way, our surroundings become sacred to us, and reflect the sacred values underlying our lives. They take on layer after layer of meaning and value to us, and become loved and inviolate in their own right. At the same time, they give power and strength to our lives and direct our actions into healthy paths. There is no way, as Chief Seattle said, we can treat our surroundings without reverence when the earth itself is composed of the ashes of our ancestors.

CHANGE FROM A *LEGAL* TO A *SACRED* BASIS FOR SOCIETY

Our society has been based on a legalistic structure – of limited commitments easy to break. In that kind of system, those embracing greed have unmatched rewards and incentives to win. As a result, endless regulations are inevitable to even partly control the damage. The only true alternative is to find a basis for our lives and actions which makes harmful action inconceivable and rare, rather than the rule. Simple regulations then are needed only to embody and convey consensus on right action. That basis for our lives must be a sacred one.

Why a *sacred* basis of society? Nothing less than that – our holding sacred the health of our surroundings and the well-being of all life – will ensure that we act strongly enough or soon enough to ensure that health and well-being.

Honor ourselves.
Honor others.
Honor all life.

When we do that, the absurdity of an agriculture based on violent and futile insecticides, herbicides, and pesticides becomes obvious, as does that of a medical system based on primary use of antibiotics to attempt to kill parts of the web of life that sustains us. We learn, rather, to deal with *causes* of the imbalances that allow unbalanced growth of one part of life.

A basis to social interaction that nurtures rather than drains, and which is tied to creating happiness rather than fighting, creates good and creates wealth for society through its process as well as its product. Its greater effectiveness in managing society's resources is merely a bonus.

LIFE WITHOUT FAILURE

Drumming is different from traditional western music – which has a *right* sequence of notes and a *right* way of playing. Once entrained by the beat, drumming leads us without conscious effort to be part of the shared rhythm, and blesses us with the inability to do wrong. With drumming or any improvisational music, variations we make within it only enrich the music and make it respond to the immediacy of time and place within which it is occurring.

The music breaks only when we fail to incorporate whatever happens into it. One 'wrong note' is an error. It stands out that we didn't mean it. But if we repeat it again – however odd it may have been – embrace it and draw it in, acknowledge it and incorporate it, it becomes part of the path of the music. It sets the participants a new challenge, and sets the music off in a new direction. A good way to approach life, too, perhaps!

All participatory music makes clear that paying to hear the best performer in the world cannot match the joy of *being part* of the making of the music, or the dance, or the song. Taking part gives pleasure – to us and to others at the same time. It gives us full-body experience, learning, and catharsis. It leaves us self-esteem rather than a feeling of inferiority and of never being able to equal the professional. It gives us the value of enjoyment, beauty, and pleasure inherent in the rhythms of life, without money, skill, or fancy equipment. What a wonderful thing, and model for life – a way of living designed for success, not failure!

Being an integral "fail-proof" part of something evolving organically and beautifully is a joyful reward whether music or the ongoing creation of all life. It gives powerful meaning and context for our lives and direction for our actions. It overturns our values of "privacy" to do our own thing without distraction from something "outside", and replaces it with enjoyment and interest in the news and activities of the family or community in which we live.

We have related to the world outside our skin as something separate from us – "others," the "environment." Yet there is no way we can be separate from the health of what surrounds us; from the air, food, life, and energy that we draw back and forth across that boundary of "our skin."

The world was not created *for* us – we are part *of* it. As much as we are "humans," we are also an incredibly complex group culture that mitochondria have developed. We are the technological innovation of rock to transport itself and give it voice. We are a creation of plants to transform the toxic oxygen wastes they release into the air back into the carbon dioxide they need for photosynthesis.

We are as well a beautiful element in the conscious body of a planet, and a local "standing wave" vortex in the energy song that generates nodes of complexity in local regions of the universe. We can see ourselves in many ways as part of nature, life, and creation. What we cannot do is to continue to see ourselves as something *apart* from nature and outside of its rules.

Like failure-proof ways of self-expression, seeing ourselves as not bound by our skins, as a part of the wonderful song of creation, can give a greater sense of meaning and worth to our lives.

As we find joy in being part of the evolving songs of life, we see the identity, attachment and meaning we have found as individuals and family expand to that of community, nation, planet, and all Creation often held in other cultures. We come to see our ancestors and descendants as part of the thread of life and giving that is our own, and to see even the stars, the rocks, and all life around us as kin.

"Fail-proof" patterns of work and relationships are inherent parts of achieving sustainability, restoring self-esteem, healing our emotional damage, and learning to honor and know our selves as a vital and integral part of life and the goals we pursue in it. A meaningful identity with the broader flows of life also enriches and deepens our self-esteem and emotional health.

VITAL RESOURCES ARE INNER ONES

Material resource limits make us again aware of the power and value of our *inner* resources. We've forgotten what many of them are - *will, courage, giving, endurance, anger, fear, love, curiosity, passion, intuition, resolution, resistance, wisdom, cunning, compulsion, restraint, joy, wit, hopefulness, rashness, caution, wonder, pride, humility, gratitude, forgiveness* – to name a few.

Use of these resources involves us *personally* in the act of creating. It gives the tangible rewards of self-esteem, confidence, and community respect for our accomplishments. In many fields, the wise use of inner resources is far more vital to accomplishment than any material resources.

These resources acknowledge that our emotions are vital dimensions of our lives coming from our hearts – dimensions to be respected and used as guides and sources of energy, not brushed aside in favor of what comes only from our heads. They acknowledge the power and value of our inherent interconnectedness with others and with all life. They connect us with magic, and the power that lies outside the limits of the rational.

The patterns of life and interaction in a sustainable community give continual reminder that we, and the resources within each of us, are one of the most vital resources of our society and planet. Our challenge is to develop them rather than ignoring them in preference for depleting material resources.

❖

NOBILITY, NOT *MOBILITY*

Our cities reflect a curious pattern of values and goals – great volumes of work spaces isolated and disconnected from true productive work; zoning-segregated and mutually contradictory fragments of lives; and above all – mobility. Mobility is a curious disease – justifiable only in allowing access to places that are different, but in the process requiring that all places become alike.

Sustainability, and the life-nurturing values upon which it is based,[10] gives us opportunity to set new goals for a society which is floundering without meaning and without direction. Equity, security, sustainability, responsibility, giving, and sacredness are its principles, and initial goals. Beyond that? Perhaps *nobility*, not mobility. Excellence. Wisdom. Harmony. Being a part of Creation and the evolution of new possibilities.

The new values, world-view, and nature of relationships in a sustainable community give opportunities and impetus to defining and attaining new and vastly more meaningful goals for society.

PEOPLE-ECONOMICS
Helping Out

Helping out is one of the most time-honored ways of dealing with services in economies that are localized enough that people know each other and are around long enough to reciprocate. It recognizes the truth of the word "obligation" – that you really owe something back to someone who has helped you that isn't erased by a mumbled "much obliged" and a round of drinks. It also acknowledges the importance in any group of *giving* – volunteering – with *no* strings attached.

Looking back, I'm amazed at how much of our lives, even in middle America, never went through the money-changers but was part of a great process of helping back and forth. Many of our vacations while growing up were to visit our relatives living in various places. One uncle was conveniently in the Army, which moved him and his family to new and exotic places like Kansas and Georgia and Virginia every two years, just so we had new places to visit them! When another of my aunts was sick, my cousin came and lived with us for several months, and our family and my uncle's took turns caring for my grandmother as she got old.

Around home, of course, money rarely changed hands for work done, so probably two-thirds of the work done by our family as a whole – like almost every family – never saw a dollar accounting. Within the neighborhood lawnmowers were borrowed, hair was cut, houses and pets taken care of during vacations, rides into town given and taken, and baby-sitting done. Our neglected grape arbor came under the wing of a neighbor lady who took the grapes every year and gave us grape juice and grape jam in return.

But dollar savings aren't the most important reward. It's often a lot easier to do things with four hands instead of two. It's usually more fun helping someone do something, where we don't have the responsibility and can just do the doing and not the worrying and figuring. It's *fun* to be in on felling trees, building walls, making things happen. It's *fun* growing new skills, learning how things are done, and what things actually are worth in sweat time, money time, and work time. And not having any skills to offer is not a problem for long. Two willing hands and a little sweat helping someone who knows how is the quickest and easiest way to learn skills.

Helping out works partly because it's all between friends, or you become friends in the process, but also because each person views the helping out very differently. The helper probably wanted an excuse to get out of the house, probably had fun helping, and probably had forgotten how desperately floundering it felt before when he or she needed that particular help themselves. The "helpees," on the other hand, think they've been given a lot more than they have, because they *needed* the help, probably didn't know how easy it was to learn or perform the assistance they were given, and probably believed the helpers knew what they were doing!

That honest and real difference in perception and valuing is an important social glue. Over a period of time and helping back and forth, it frequently ends up with everyone feeling they've gotten back a whole lot more than they've given themselves. I have that feeling of gratitude and thanks towards many of our neighbors and friends, and have discovered that many feel the same in reverse. The used water heater we were given saved a trip to the dump for our neighbor, but to us it was the equivalent of $100 and the heart of a future solar water system. And so it goes.

In any case, most helping out is just that. It rarely is tied to getting something back, though eventually things come full circle through the oddest of routes.

One of the great benefits of economics where people do matter is that they force you to get to know people and get to understand people. You have to learn that George won't ever turn down your request for help, though his back is killing him this week, and you shouldn't ask him. Or that Alice has a wealth of skills for cutting bureaucratic red tape. And that Sam is always dependable in a pinch. And somewhere along the line, you begin to learn the true costs – both economic and social – of an economics where people don't matter.

Haggling
The necessity of people-economics may lie in the future, but its benefits are available now and being sought by more and more people as the novelty of our supermarket culture dissolves into a bitter aftertaste of exploitation. Just one step away from the new car showroom is the used car lot, beyond the edge of the safe and standardized world and into a fluid and ever-changing world whose rewards require an expenditure of your personal energy. You're on your own! Buying and selling used things – cars, clothes, houses or whatever – requires more knowledge and gambling to participate in, but also offers greater returns for that risk and effort. Haggling is the most common people-process for determining price for goods in a particular situation.

Some years ago, when we moved to Oregon, we bought a used cookstove for $50. We were novices to the world of used goods, and didn't know if we were being taken, but it was worth the risk for the time we needed it. After our house burned down, we went back to the same place, because by then we knew they'd been fair and honest. They didn't have any stoves of the kind we wanted, but told us we really couldn't go wrong with *any* used stove we could find. They either work or they don't, and they're easy to fix.

When we finally found one, the guy wanted $40 for it, but didn't have any place to plug it in to see if it worked. We knew by then that the price was great if it worked, and probably fair if it needed fixing. When we got it home and plugged it in, sparks flew everywhere. The problem boiled down to one broken wire and less than an hour to fix. Cheap new stoves cost over $200, so we ended up with a better product, saved about 75 percent of the cost, and learned how to repair a stove – a good return for asking a few questions and taking a small gamble.

Second-hand stores, auctions, used car lots, classified ads, friends, and haggling prices are all a different kind of economics than strip malls and big-box retailers. Price depends on what you know and don't know, how you and the other person feel towards each other, how much others are willing to pay and what you really want it for. Do a little homework – check prices in the classifieds, look up new prices in a catalog. Talk to a repair person. Get a feel for the market. It takes a little more time and asking the right questions. It develops a good eye for people.

One of my first lessons in barter, when I couldn't even speak or read the language, came from a fellow-traveler in Istanbul when we were buying food from the market vendors. "Stand back and watch the coins," he said. See what the locals are paying for what, even if you don't know the language. The second lesson – don't insult the seller or the merchandise if you don't know what you're talking about. The bluff is obvious, insulting, and infuriating. Just say you aren't willing to spend that much money for that merchandise, and make a counter-offer. Compare prices and condition, and play from there.

Yes, haggling takes a little time, but it's a cheap and worthwhile education. It leads to respect for the other person, how much they know, and how well they can size you up. It adds a human dimension to an exchange. It is probably the only practical way to deal with the trading of unique or used goods, and a source of fun and satisfaction that cannot be gotten from buying fixed-price new merchandise. When fewer and fewer of us can afford "new," it's a rewarding, cash- and resource-effective way to trade, and truly part of an economics where people *do* matter.

Passing It On

It seems immediate, on having a baby, that packages begin arriving in the mail, continuing an age-old custom. They each contain a hodge-podge of new and used baby clothes – some well-worn and handed on from birth to birth; others special memorabilia kept for several generations and stored away carefully until needed. Some are new-bought, crisp and bright; some hand-made by friends and grandmothers who knew of special needs and loves. We know of people who buy such things all new. At one time we might have been more inclined that way ourselves. But the patient love that some forgotten grandmother several generations ago put into a tiny lace collar wouldn't be there. And the special pleasures of thinking of the friend who made a quilt or crocheted a crazy hat; or of having baby clothes made from remnants left over from your own favorite high school shirt can't be bought in any store at any price.

This simple and ancient custom of *passing on* is much more than a wise and welcome frugality. It's a part of our economics where *people do matter* – never making the slightest blip in our GNP, but making much welcomed gifts to our hearts and lives.

Our money economy is well and intentionally designed so that people don't matter. Jobs are designed so that people are easily replaceable and therefore less valuable and lower paid. Goods are designed to be disposable. Along with them we dispose of some of the self-respect of the people who worked long hours to make them. Products are designed and packaged to prevent a buyer from finding out the durability or details of construction or operation. Products are merchandised at fixed prices so salespeople and buyers cannot exercise and develop judgement of what is an appropriate price for a given situation. Yet the merchandiser is free to scoot the prices up or down to lure or soak the buyer.

Little is said about parts of our economy where people *do* matter – there's no profit to be made in promoting someone else's self-reliance. But passing things on, auctions, barter, helping our friends, self-reliance, and household economics all have an increasingly important role to play in our future. For that future has to restore the sense of human and natural dignity, of belonging, and of psychological and spiritual reward of life that have been destroyed by our industrial economic culture.[11]

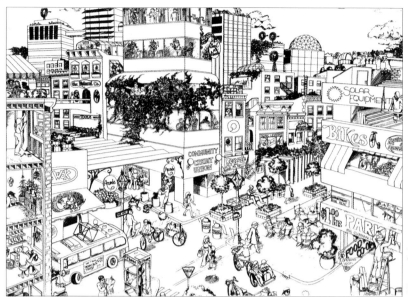

Diane Schatz

Urban areas are being reinvented as well as suburban ones. Energy-efficiency retrofits, car-sharing, covered pedestrian ways, public transit, rooftop gardens are all contributing to cityscapes where life and community can be convenient and enjoyable.

SUBURBAN RENEWAL

We sat down a number of years ago to brainstorm what would be involved in conversion of suburbs to a saner, more conserving way of life. The news was good. *It's easier to get simpler than to get wasteful!* The space-grabbing demands of the automobile required whole new urban and regional infrastructures. Adapting to its wiser use requires only ingenuity and self-interest, which we've never been short on. We got our friend Diane Schatz to draw up some of the possibilities:

> * *Intensive gardening* and Tender Loving Care (TLC) in suburban gardens has been shown in England to actually *increase* food output per acre. The Farallones Integral Urban House in Berkeley and other projects across the U.S. have similarly shown a very substantial part of a household's food needs can be met with very little space or labor. Fruit and nut-bearing trees can provide both food and natural air-conditioning in the summer. Might as well get some food out of all the yard work that many people do! Our main concern should be to avoid poisoning the ground and future crops grown on it.

Less expensive accommodation of population. Water, power, streets, sewers, phone and other utilities are already in place in suburbia. Improved efficiency means many more families can be served by the existing utility networks. Some possibilities:

> – Conversion of large suburban homes to duplexes or apartments. Many have multiple baths, would convert easily and would provide a better retirement investment than pensions.

> – Street houses and backyard apartments. Closure of unnecessary streets can provide opportunities to build additional housing or neighborhood gardens in their place. Conversion of garages to apartments puts existing structures to more productive uses.

Public transit becomes possible where doubling of the use of existing housing, utility networks and roads increases the density. *Neighborhood shopping* becomes more feasible with more people within walking or bicycling distance of a shop.

Home businesses are already becoming more common, in spite of prohibitive zoning regulations. Conversion of garages to businesses, home workshops to furniture making and repair, and spare bedrooms to home offices is occurring more and more frequently as people discover working patterns that eliminate commuting, that can be started themselves with minimum capital, and that provide rewarding and secure work. Renting guest rooms provides a low-cost alternative to freeway motels.

Neighborhood or community-sized renewable energy systems can augment individual conservation and solar systems at less cost than conventional power plants. Solar collectors on the roof of shared parking, laundry, or shop space, connected to large heat storage tanks serving a whole block, are already coming off the drawing boards, and community wind-electric systems are now operational.

These changes are already happening. What already exists in suburbia can be used much more intensely, creatively and effectively. What needs change is our habits and our patterns – the physical environment can be adapted quite readily.[12]

THE THIRD PIG IS ALWAYS FATTEST

A friend, many years ago, told us the story of The Third Pig. A series of experiments were made in China, feeding one pig normal food, feeding a second pig only on the undigested food passed through the first pig's digestive system, feeding a third pig only on the unabsorbed food in the feces of the second pig, and so on. *Amazingly, the third pig was always fattest!* Enzymes in the digestive tracts of the first two pigs converted normally unavailable food into forms that could be absorbed by the third pig. The Third Pig is a useful image for a society that knows how to cleverly take advantage of the value remaining in cast-off wastes.

We've been a First Pig Society – getting everything custom-made to our specifications, yet less wealthy than we seem, because we have to pay the high costs of providing exactly what we demand and again to get rid of our unwanted wastes. Such trash still has a lot of the value originally put into it – a discarded water heater may have just been too small, or the element failed but the tank was still good. Junkyard autos still have may good parts, or at least are a resource of excellent alloy metals.

It takes different skills and resourcefulness to match our dreams to what can be made from what's available, just as it takes different enzymes to release the food value remaining in our food wastes. But those skills allow a person or society to take advantage of work already done and they make living cheaper and easier. Looking back to growing up in small-town America, I was always puzzled why the junkman drove the biggest Cadillac in town – now maybe I understand!

A First Pig Society cuts forests to make paper from wood pulp, then incinerates the used paper. A Second Pig Society uses slash from logging to produce paper, and recovers energy from burning the waste-paper. A Third Pig Society makes paper *from* waste material. In India, handmade paper is made from jute – but not jute grown for paper. They take old gunny sacks that are no longer usable as such – cut them up, boil with caustic soda, reduce to pulp and make paper. Similarly, paper made from bamboo does not come from bamboo groves cultivated to make paper. Rather, wild bamboo is made into mats and baskets. They are used, and last five or ten years. When they fall apart and are cast aside, the broken baskets and mats are taken from the waste heaps and used to make paper.

Our food wastes can be flushed down the sewer. Or they can be made into compost to fertilize our gardens. Or they can be fed to pigs to produce pork before they are made into compost for the gardens. Or some of them can be used for soup stock before being fed to pigs. Each time a new level of use is slipped into the stream of wastes, we take additional advantage of the work that nature and people performed to produce the amazing interlocked patterns of materials and energy that make up our world. Each level of reuse, repair, and recycling that we ignore means more work to create from scratch the products we could obtain from the waste materials.

A Third Pig Society is not a poor society eking out its survival from scrounging waste heaps. It is, rather, a wise and wealthy society – one that recognizes that the maxims of "Highest and Best Use" and "Use the Work Already Done" make for a better life than "Start from Scratch."[13]

DOWN IN THE DUMPS

People often are startled when my wife says she runs the dump. *"Why would anyone . . ."* The town dump isn't the cleanest and easiest place to work. But it, like every piece of our communities, can be transformed from what it has been. And that's exactly what she and her group, Cart'M, has done. Even though we're over a hundred miles

A new sink for a couple of dollars? Who is happier – the buyer, or the previous owner who finally got it out of their garage?

Shopping at the dump is a combination of treasure hunt, "Name That Thing," and community gathering. It's not searching for a bargain – everything is a bargain. It's looking for the impossible and unexpected, and finding it . . . with a little help from some friends.

from any recycling markets, they have added an ever-more-comprehensive recycling center to the dump. And then a resale store, where things no longer wanted by one person can be passed on to another. Those are the major pieces we would see from a material standpoint.

But from a community energy standpoint, it has been done in a way that is even more transformative. Just adding the retail store emptied out half of the mini-storage buildings, and doubled the size of many people's garages as they let go of the physical and emotional weight of huge piles of things they didn't need, but which were "too good to throw away." If they do need something later that they got rid of, they can probably find it, or someone else's, in the resale store.

When Lane started calling it "The Dump" again, people would get a funny grin. No bureaucratic "Material Recovery Transfer Facility (MRTF)" nonsense – just the dump. That's what we've always called it, that's what it *is*. It's *ours*. "Trash art" workshops, a yearly trash art show and party changed the energy even further. Last year's attracted 1000 people, dancing among the dumpsters!

Staffed by over 75 volunteers in addition to paid staff, the dump has become a wonderful community place. People doing "community service" from the courts stay on as volunteers, because it feels so wonderful working with people who are doing something good. Prices in the store are so cheap (have to make room for more stuff coming in) that people coming in after a house fire have gotten a whole house outfitted with beds, appliances, furniture and eating utensils for less than $100. All kinds of people, that normally don't get to know each other, rub shoulders and figure out how to make something work. In the process, people who need a hug, or feel "down in the dumps," can get a hug and a few words connecting them with what they need.

Mini-industries, using the dump as raw material for local-use products, such as compost from yard debris, greenhouses from recycled windows, resurrected bicycles, and lawn mowers are beginning to develop. People bring their visitors to the dump . . . it's become a tourist attraction. Changing the dump has improved resource productivity. But more, it has changed the our energy about "stuff," waste, involvement, and enjoyment – and brought community to life, in the process.

The "informal" sector of our economy is probably the biggest element ignored in conventional economics. It is an invisible world of all that doesn't pass through money transactions, a world which dwarfs the money economy. Large as it is, its quantitative neglect is less important than its *qualitative* absence in our lives as more and more becomes monetized.

The informal sector is where people *do* matter; where more than just money moves back and forth in transactions; where respect, caring, confidence and community are the interchange and the product. Curitiba shows us its importance in community, and what it makes possible. Give it room, and it will bring life. Don't waste your time trying to measure it, but see its power in the balance. Let its sense of wholeness shift how we approach all parts of our lives.

[1] SMALL IS BEAUTIFUL, E.F. Schumacher, Harper & Row, 1974.
[2] *"Work and Leisure,"* Tom Bender, MANAS, April 1983.
[3] *"Let Fantasies Be Fantasies,"* Tom Bender, RAIN Magazine, April 1977.
[4] *"Jobs, Humbug!"* Tom Bender, RAIN Magazine, April 1978.
[5] from *"Unexpected Gifts,"* Tom Bender, 1996.
[6] See my *"Sewage is Art - The Healing of Place with Chi"*, June 1995, for what happens when we apply this to a building project.
[7] See my *"Shedding a Skin That No Longer Fits"*, March 1996, for a deeper discussion.
[8] See my *"Sacred Roots of Sustainable Design"*, Sept. 1995.

[9] See HEART OF PLACE, above.

[10] See my SHARING SMALLER PIES, 1975. *"New Values"* section reprinted in RAIN, April 1975; NEW AGE JOURNAL, Nov. 1975; THE FUTURIST, 1976; RESETTLING AMERICA, Gary Coates, ed. Brick House, 1981. Excerpted in UTNE READER, Fall 1987. See also *"Shedding a Skin..."* above.

[11] from *"Economics Where People DO Matter,"* Tom Bender, RAIN Magazine, April 1979.

[12] *"Suburban Renewal,"* Tom Bender, RAIN Magazine, April 1978.

[13] *"The Third Pig is Always Fattest,"* Tom Bender, RAIN, May, 1977.

Chapter 10
New Measures of Success

Efficiency, resource productivity and economics are part of a complex, multidimensional web of culture and ecology. Effects of decisions may be far removed in time, space, and connection. Work patterns that drive a person crazy have *that* as a delayed and significant cost. If, in their craziness, that person becomes a terrorist, the costs become an order of magnitude greater. A decision that seems wise in itself, but which ultimately leads to war, has profound costs that were never in the original calculus. Sustainability has cultural and spiritual dimensions as well as technological and ecological. Factor Ten economic changes can be used merely for consumption of more material goods, or as we've seen, used to restore wholeness, meaning, and long-term benefit for all.

THE RESACRALIZATION OF LIFE

The role of spirit and religion, and of goals which include our relation with the divine play a unique and poorly understood role in achieving that well-being. Islam began, for example, not to create a new religion but a healthy community centered on *justice*, *equity* and *compassion*. Seeing the dangers of concentration of wealth in his community, Mohammed insisted it was wrong to build a private fortune, but good to share wealth and create a society where the weak and vulnerable were treated with respect.

This concern is echoed in the Hindu culture in India, where the measure of a person's wealth and status is not what they've hoarded, but what they are able to give away. Similarly in the American Pacific Northwest, the *potlatch* giveaway of wealth was considered a measure of a person's true power. A person who has given all away, and has the personal capacity – as perhaps a good hunter or leader – to generate new wealth, is respected more and has more to contribute to their community than one who merely inherited or hoarded wealth or obtained it through a fluke. Both were cultural mechanisms developed to redistribute wealth and create the equity essential for viable community, while tying status and prestige directly with ability and achievement rather than greed or inheritance.

Muslims were commanded, as their prime duty, to build a community (*ummah*) in which there was a fair distribution of wealth. This was considered far more important than any abstruse theological doctrines. The political and social welfare of the community therefore held sacramental value for Muslims, and the goal of Islam was to resolve the spiritual malaise, chronic and destructive warfare, and injustice that violated their community beliefs. Interestingly, Mohammed insisted there be no coercion in matters of faith, and commanded Muslims to respect as equal the beliefs of Jews and Christians. Ultimately, Mohammed managed to break the chronically violent cycles of Arabic tribal warfare, vendetta and counter-vendetta, and bring peace to wartorn Arabia through expanding his community based on justice, equity and compassion.[1]

I am no great friend of religion – but spirit has transformed my life and that of all I know whom it has touched. All the great religions began with a mystic – an individual directly in touch with spirit and bringing its wisdom into the lives of their community. Christ, Mohammed, Buddha, LaoTsu – all said, *"Don't make a religion out of me."* They knew that spirit can be, and must be, touched directly in our own lives. As their wisdom spread in each of their cultures, large religious institutions formed – from very honest desires. Still with mystics, yes. But inevitably with administrators also, who ultimately took control of the religion, and again and again banned and expelled the mystics and practices whose experience they couldn't equal, understand, or convey.

Yet spontaneous and direct spiritual experience plays a vital role in individual, community, and cultural health. Contemporary records of the spiritual ecstasy in France at the time of the building of the Gothic cathedrals appear unbelievable from a secular viewpoint.[2] But the miraculous occurrences that grew out of entire communities embracing the concepts of confession and penance, the forgiving of enemies, and humility with obedience, fit precisely with those in different traditions from the Maya in MesoAmerica[3] to the Dagara in Africa,[4] to Islam in the Arabic world.[5]

Religion, at its worst, is a stifling burden on our lives and culture. At its best, as we've seen with Mohammed's transformation of Arabic politics and the spiritual communities of the Middle Ages, it can be a powerful and highly "economic" tool for community well-being. I dwell on it here, because religion and spirit, and its role in culture and economics is the most central issue we face today.

RELIGIOUS FUNDAMENTALISM

The separation of spiritual and secular culture in the last century was probably unavoidable in testing and evolving more successful cultural patterns. It has led to extremely serious and explosive conditions, warfare, and terrorism, but also to a deeper understanding of the need to reintegrate spirit, culture, and economics. Religious fundamentalism has surfaced in *every* nation and *every* major faith in response to deep dissatisfaction with failures of modern culture. It has arisen as a fight for personal, cultural, religious and spiritual survival; from deep and justified fears of the exclusion of the divine from public life; and as a desperate attempt to make spiritual values prevail in the modern world. It has arisen in response to a culture which is rightfully seen as having no light, no heart and no spirituality.

Religious fundamentalism itself has often been twisted into negative and violent forms by those same tendencies of modern culture. Whatever its other value, fundamentalism *has* been successful in bringing religious and spiritual issues from the sidelines back to center field in the political arena.

We've seen the essential need and merit of spiritual values in transforming our understanding of work and other aspects of economics, and in achieving personal and cultural health. We've seen their importance in helping us develop major new effectiveness in our institutions and industry, and in finding deeper personal and social goals and more direct and economic means of attaining them.

Ours is a time of gathering in, of winnowing and reintegrating the wisdom of different ages and different cultures, of relinking the material and the transcendent in our lives. Both in spite of and because of the secularism of modern culture, we are compelled today to reforge those transcendent dimensions of life; rediscover the mechanisms by which we, as every culture, can directly and personally access them; and achieve their reintegration into our economic life.

As Islam and other spiritual traditions have kept to the forefront of consciousness for centuries, the concepts of social justice, equality, tolerance and practical compassion come from spirit. They have immense practical application in our lives. Spiritual laws, ecological laws, social laws are all one in a viable, mature society. An economics of wholeness must include resacralization of our lives and culture, becoming one which can both heal and generate immense new growth to our culture.

WE SUCCEED WHEN *ALL* SUCCEED

One intriguing aspect of this economics is totally alien to our customary ways of thinking yet holds enormous potential for our future. That is the "giveability" of many of the possibilities and productivity leaps it engenders. Information, knowledge, and wisdom are a kind of wealth that need not be hoarded like money. They can all be given away and shared freely without depleting what *we* have – in fact often enhancing our knowledge or wisdom in the process.

Education resources, as mentioned above, can be broadcast worldwide for virtually the same cost of broadcasting them to one state or region. Shared worldwide, and used year after year, they represent 100-fold cost savings, and most simply can be given *free*.

The wisdom of building a high-efficiency refrigerator or light bulb manufacturing plant rather than five electrical power plants to supply energy for inefficient lights and refrigerators is merely newly perceived common sense. That kind of common sense is applicable *everywhere*, and can dramatically lessen our demands. Sharing those perceptions – and their demonstrated benefits – with others costs little, yet reaps enormous benefits.

The impressive savings possible from stabilizing populations, rather than continuing massive investments to accommodate more people, are available – and needed – in every country of the world. The benefits of equity are a lesson of particular value to over-industrialized countries, but applicable to all. And massive inequity is not unknown in even the poorest countries. The costs of debt make it a wise thing for *all* to avoid. Coupling such new perceptions with actions to embody them in our own lives gives an irresistible impetus to others to act similarly.

Our future is inexorably linked with the health and well-being of all people and all life. These questions have shown that we *can* easily reduce our own excessive demands for the limited resources of our planet. We can reduce them easily to levels which *can* be sustained for all, while restoring the health of the rest of the biosphere. Through them, both our own quality of life and that of everyone on the planet can be significantly improved within those same limits of sustainability.

TEN EASY PIECES OF A BETTER WORLD[6]

The September 11 terrorist bombings in New York and Washington D.C. are bringing a new search for patterns of living that reflect our highest capabilities and aspirations for all of humanity and all life on Earth. "Patriotism," David Spangler says, "is aligning ourselves with the Soul of America, seeking to embody in our everyday lives the *highest* of what it means to be an American. That is the kind of patriotism we need today. A spirit which reflects the vastness and energy of our land, the spirit of all the races and peoples who live here, the spiritual powers that nurture all humanity. Love, courage, openness, discovery, creativity, tolerance, and freedom. Honoring equality, individuality and difference – and using these forces to create a greater whole through willing cooperation. The true Spirit of America is a gift we can give to the rest of the world, whose light can outshine a past of greed and violence." That spirit needs a different way of manifesting than the economics upon which we have centered our culture.

Our deepest goals are rarely material or economic. They include love and being loved, feeling of value to others, knowing we have something to contribute. They embrace friendship, peace, security, health, well-being, adventure, joy, passion and spirit. They encompass meaningfulness and purpose of our life; growth, fullness, and experience; successful meeting of challenges; knowledge and expansion of our own capabilities. It's time to remember and embrace those goals – for our entire global family. They can change the world:

1. End terrorism – Let's start with our own actions, and permanently dismantle our hated "School of the Americas" terrorist training center in Georgia, and any similar institutions. End our assassinations of foreign leaders and support of repressive regimes. (We have assassinated at least 8 foreign leaders in the last 50 years, and Presidents Clinton and Bush have acknowledged at least four attempts to kill bin Laden.) Stop our sales of 68% of the weapons sold to developing countries. End our embargo against civilian Iraq which has already resulted in over 100,000 innocent Iraqi children dead of slow starvation. Let's continue to seek, as we have, international rather than unilateral action in response to acts of terrorism. Let's bring the individuals and organizations accused before impartial international justice, not just bomb them into oblivion. Any party to a conflict can make a persuasive case for their position and actions. We need to hear all sides, and to extend to others our judicial beliefs of "innocent until proved guilty." It is the only position that can lead to true justice and to respect before the world. Let's reduce the causes of terrorism, and join together internationally to deal with the fanatics that remain.

2. *Achieve energy independence* – Domestic energy sources continue to decline. Our dependence on imports increases, and with it our trade imbalances and entanglements such as Vietnam, Libya, Iraq, the Persian Gulf, and now Afghanistan. Solar and energy efficiency can reduce building and industrial energy use 90%, saving money as well. Accelerated introduction of "Hypercars" can replace our existing vehicle fleet with 100mpg cars in five years. We can reduce our oil need 90% in five years. Get our economy moving – fine – but lets do it by producing things that make a *real* difference. Busses, not bombs; high-speed trains, not airline bailouts; homes ten times as efficient as today's.

3. *Get out of debt* – Foreign debts and draconian measures to bring debtor countries into unfair trade agreements are one of the root causes of international anger against our "global" culture. Forgiving debts we knew would lead to such results is an essential first step. Getting out of debt at home individually, as businesses, and as a nation is the same as increasing our incomes by 20% – what we all pay for interest charges. Pledge that 20% to help the rest of the world.

4. *Require fair wages* – People are starving even in our own country. It is criminal to me to allow a person to be paid a wage less than one third of a minimum "living wage." Triple the minimum wage, locally or nationally, and reduce government aid spending in the process. Tax the wealthy to restore economic equity. Equity, practical compassion, and social justice are the cornerstones of Muslim culture. Can't we do as much?

5. *Establish fair trade* – "Free trade" is freedom only for the powerful to exploit the poor. It allows moving money and resources, but doesn't allow people to move where wages or living conditions are better. Its results are not justified – transfer of more wealth to the wealthy, at the expense of the poor. Turn GATT and NAFTA upside down. Our trade agreements need to be public and democratic, not secret; determined by sovereign governments, not private corporations; judicated by impartial public bodies, not the corporations themselves; and supportive of fair wages, environmental health, local autonomy,

and improving quality of life – everywhere. Dismantle the World Bank and the International Monetary Fund which have been instrumental in destroying the autonomous economy of country after country, and replace them with institutions enabling each country to develop their own way of life.

6. Stabilize our population, help others stabilize theirs – Growth is the root source of so many of our world problems. We now spend 33-40% of our national income to pay for growth. Think what a difference those resources could make in other people's lives.

7. Share with others – We have more than is fair. Some of it can be shared with the rest of the world with no loss to ourselves. Stabilizing growth, improving equity, and reducing debt can maintain our present well-being with 80% less resources. Couldn't we share a big part of that to improve the well-being of others?

8. Help everyone achieve local food self-sufficiency – This is basic. Without it, people are forced into terms of trade they have no power to affect, and further impoverishment. With it comes power to determine their own lives, culture, and relationship with others.

9. Stop discounting the future – If we want a positive future, we need to understand what comprises and generates that future, and take the steps to achieve it. A central element of our economics has been discounting the future – analytically and in real life. We already live in that future, have received significant reduction in our well-being, and are faced now with a future of strife, terrorism, reduction in civil liberties, global warming and pain. An economics of wholeness, which shows true costs and doesn't discount the future, can produce ten-fold improvement in our entire economy. Evaluation of CEOs based on achieving long-term benefits rather than immediate resource liquidation can align business practices with public good. As farmers say, "Don't eat your seed corn."

10. Restore values and the sacred to our lives and culture – Start on the street. Every purchase we make is based on deceit. Prices that make us think we're paying less than we are, packaging that confuses and makes comparison difficult, hidden financing costs, manipulative advertising. Honest and helpful pricing can restore respect to our transactions. Take sex and body parts off of our magazine covers and out of our ads. It offends, degrades, exploits basic human nature. It perverts, corrupts and debases the wonder and beauty of sex, love, passion, and beauty into a tool to deceive us yet again. In traditional Japan, nudity and mixed bathing were commonplace, but photographs of naked people considered obscene. Intention and exploitation are offensive, not how much of our bodies are covered. In the aftermath of September 11, people are suddenly offended by advertising. Feel in yourself why that is so, and remember advertising raises prices of many products by another 20%.

A path away from terrorism is possible. It arises most often from a history of true injustice. The August, 2001 interview with former U.S. Attorney General Ramsey Clark in *The Sun* indicates that our culture has caused some of that injustice.[7] Our path begins by taking steps to put people before profit, caring before greed, justice, equity and compassion before all else. It is amazing that we are finding at this very time the means to transform our economics and with it to make the whole world a success.

WHEN OUR HEARTS DO TOUCH

As the examples in this book show, we are already letting loose of old ways and moving into a transformed world. We see the discord between how we've lived and the values that underlie our lives. We sense a thread of new rightness which can buoy, connect and direct our lives. We're rediscovering authentic community. A familiar feeling wells up in a book about South African Archbishop Desmund TuTu:

> *"We Africans speak about a concept difficult to render in English. We speak of UBUNTU or BOTHO. You know when it is there, and it is obvious when it is absent. It has to do with what it means to be truly human. It refers to gentleness, to compassion, to hospitality, to openness to others, to vulnerability, to be available for others and to know that you are bound up with them in the bundle of life, for a person is only a person through other persons."[8]*

These very characteristics distinguish what it is like to live in a world, and by an economics, of wholeness – in absolute contrast to the characteristics of life in a world of greed and self-centeredness. They are also the identical things we feel in others and ourselves when we relate in ways which empower all concerned.

When we look in awe at the achievements in South Africa, in Curitiba or Gaviotas, or on the steppes of Mongolia, we know that miracles do exist – that we *can* achieve the impossible and create for ourselves and the whole world a future worth living for.

Our lives, our institutions, and our communities can live lightly on the earth, can be in harmony with all life, and can create a better future for all of us on this planet.

We belong to the world. We belong to life. It is a glorious thing to behold and *be* part of the ongoing creation of life. We are finding that the Creation of which we are part is even more awesome than ever imagined. Casting our lives into the balance on the side of life – of becoming and being a part of the on-going evolution of new, more unexpected, and ever more wonderful combinations of life – is a future to brighten all of our dreams.

---

[1] I'm deeply indebted to Karen Armstrong, and her ISLAM: A Short History, Modern Library, 2000, for her insightful and compassionate scholarship on Islam and on modern religious fundamentalism.

[2] For quoted passages, see CHARTRES AND THE BIRTH OF THE CATHEDRAL, Titus Burckhardt, 1962. English translation World Wisdom Books, 1996.

[3] MAYA COSMOS, David Freidel, Linda Schele, and Joy Parker. Wm. Morrow & Co, 1993.

[4] Malidoma Somé, OF WATER AND THE SPIRIT, Tarcher/Putnam, 1994; THE HEALING WISDOM OF AFRICA, Tarcher/Putnam, 1998; RITUAL, Swan/Raven & Co, 1993.

[5] See Armstrong, above, particularly on Al-Ghazzali, Sufism, and the development of a profound level of inner spiritual resonance in Islamic institutions from political and community to worker guilds.

[6] "Ten Easy Pieces of a Better World," Tom Bender, Guest Column, DAILY ASTORIAN, Oct. 31, 2001.

[7] "Neighborhood Bully: Ramsey Clark On American Militarism," Derrick Jensen, THE SUN, August, 2001. Also, Jonathan Kwitney's ENDLESS ENEMIES: The Making of an Unfriendly World, Penguin, 1986.

[8] TUTU: ARCHBISHOP WITHOUT FRONTIERS, Shirley DuBoulay, Hodder & Stoughton, 1996.

Appendix A
Checklist for Whole-Systems Economics

I. ROOT GOALS

☐ WORK WITH SPIRITUAL FRAMEWORKS AND ECONOMIC SYSTEMS WHICH ARE CONGRUENT

☐ SEEK *REAL* WEALTH

☐ MEET GLOBAL NEEDS WITH WASTED RESOURCES

☐ ACHIEVE EQUITY OF WEALTH ESSENTIAL TO FULFILLMENT OF POTENTIALS

☐ ENSURE SUSTAINABILITY

☐ SEEK *WISDOM*, NOT INFORMATION; SHARE KNOWLEDGE WITH ALL

☐ REPLENISH NATURAL SYSTEMS

☐ DON'T LOSE WHAT WE CAN'T REPLACE

☐ DON'T NEED IT – DON'T FIGHT FOR IT

☐ AVOID NEEDS

☐ HONOR THE TRADITIONAL WISDOM OF ALL CULTURES

☐ LOOK FOR THE *REAL* REWARDS WE SEEK

☐ BUILD ON SUSTAINABLE VALUES

☐ SEEK SPIRITUAL CONNECTION WITH OUR SURROUNDINGS, OTHER CULTURES, AND NATURAL SYSTEMS

☐ PROVIDE THE WEALTH OF REWARDING WORK

☐ CHOOSE ACTIONS AND ECONOMICS THAT SUSTAIN OUR RE-LATION WITH OTHER PEOPLE AND THE REST OF LIFE

☐ TOUCH THE SPIRIT OF WHERE WE LIVE

☐ CONNECT US WITH THE STARS

☐ NURTURE INNER RESOURCES

☐ CREATE PLACES FOR OUR HEARTS AND MINDS

☐ SEEK WHAT DRAWS FORTH LOVE

☐ GIVE THE UNEXPECTED!

☐ EMBRACE THE SACREDNESS OF ALL CREATION

☐ HONOR LIFE, AND THE POWER THAT BEGETS IT

☐ GIVE OUR SPIRITS HOMES

☐ HONOR THINGS

☐ CONNECT US TO THE LIFE AROUND US

II. PREPARING OURSELVES

☐ ASSUME WE REALLY DON'T KNOW WHAT WE'RE DOING

☐ WORK FROM A CONVICTION THAT WE *CAN* ACHIEVE *MAGNITUDES* OF CHANGE

☐ THINK INTEGRATIVELY AND ECOLOGICALLY

☐ THINK OUTSIDE OF THE BOX

☐ ASSUME ANYTHING THAT COMES TO MIND CAN BE PART OF A POTENTIAL SOLUTION

☐ EXAMINE MULTIPLE-REWARD SYSTEMS, SUCH AS GIVING AND SHARING

☐ BREAK RULES

☐ USE LATERAL AND BRIDGE THINKING

☐ LOOK FOR THE *HEART* ISSUES BENEATH THE *HEAD* ONES

☐ REMEMBER THAT GOAL AND PROCESS ARE ONE

☐ REPLACE MATERIAL AND ENERGY RESOURCES WITH IN-SIGHT AND INGENUITY

☐ TOUCH THE HEART OF ALL WE MAKE

☐ EXPERIENCE CHI ENERGY

III. INTEGRATED SYSTEMS DESIGN

☐ *AVOID* PROBLEMS RATHER THAN SOLVE THEM

☐ LOOK FOR *BIG* CHANGES IN PATTERNS, NOT FINE-TUNING OF EXISTING ELEMENTS

☐ BUILD FOR ETERNITY

☐ FIND ACTIONS THAT YIELD MULTIPLE BENEFITS

☐ REMEMBER PRINCIPLES OF SUSTAINABLE SYSTEMS ARE OF-TEN THE INVERSE OF GROWTH SYSTEMS

☐ MINIMIZE TRUE LIFECYCLE COSTS

☐ KNOW THE *TRUE* COSTS

☐ *ASSUME* ROOM FOR ORDER-OF-MAGNITUDE IMPROVEMENT IN ANY SYSTEM NOT PREVIOUSLY EXAMINED

☐ SEEK SOLUTIONS THAT INCREASE SECURITY AND STABILITY

☐ LET NATURE DO IT

☐ FIND THE PRIMARY GOALS OF THE SYSTEM

☐ SEEK SOLUTIONS SATISFYING TO *ALL* INVOLVED

☐ FOCUS ON SERVICE FLOWS, NOT PRODUCT.

☐ VIEW POLLUTION OR WASTE PRODUCTS AS *RESOURCES* OUT OF PLACE.

☐ ELIMINATE PROFIT

☐ ACKNOWLEDGE WHAT YOU SEE

☐ DON'T ACCEPT ECONOMIC, ACCOUNTING, AND REGULA- TORY CONVENTIONS

IV. ECOLOGICAL SYSTEM CHARACTERISTICS

☐ CLOSE LOOPS

☐ OPTIMIZE EMBRACING SYSTEMS RATHER THAN EMBEDDED ONES

☐ TRACK THE ENERGY FLOWS

☐ LOOK AT EXPENDITURES AS *COSTS*

☐ LOOK FOR THE MULTIPLE ELEMENTS WHICH MAKE UP TRUE SOLUTIONS TO ANY PROBLEM

☐ SEEK SOLUTIONS THAT SOLVE MULTIPLE PROBLEMS

☐ USE ECOLOGICAL ECONOMICS (1+1=3)

☐ AVOID INTERMEDIARIES

☐ CONSIDER ADDING INTERMEDIARIES

V. FINE TUNING

☐ REMEMBER LOVINS' "GET THE SEQUENCE RIGHT"

☐ SEEK PATTERNS THAT *ELIMINATE* NEED FOR OTHER ELEMENTS

☐ EFFICIENCY IN IMPORTANT THINGS IS MORE SIGNIFICANT THAN IN UNIMPORTANT THINGS

☐ LOOK FOR THE BENEFITS OF *DISTRIBUTED* INTELLIGENCE AND RESPONSIBILITY IN A SYSTEM

☐ MINIMIZE SECONDARY AND MANAGERIAL WORK

☐ AVOID SIZE WHERE POSSIBLE

☐ MAKE WHERE WE *ARE* PARADISE!

☐ REINVENT WHAT EXISTS

☐ LOOK FOR SOLUTIONS THAT TAKE ADVANTAGE OF LOCAL CONDITIONS

☐ AVOID AND COUNTER EFFECTS OF ADVERTISING

☐ LIVE SIMPLY, WORK LESS

☐ AVOID SOLUTIONS THAT TRANSFER RATHER THAN REDUCE COSTS

☐ REPLACE MATERIAL AND ENERGY RESOURCES AND WORK WITH INFORMATION

☐ REPLACE INFORMATION WITH WISDOM

Appendix B
Value Shifts for
Whole-Systems Economics

NEW VALUES[1]

Our ability to develop a culture that can endure beyond our own lifetimes depends upon our coming to a new understanding of what is desirable for a harmonious and sustainable relationship with the systems that support our lives.

STEWARDSHIP, not progress.

We have valued progress highly during our period of growth, as we have known that changes were unavoidable, and have needed an orientation that could help us adjust to and assist those changes. Progress assumes that the future will be better - which at the same time creates dissatisfaction with the present and tells us that now isn't as good. As a result, we are prompted to work harder to get what the future can offer, but lose our ability to enjoy what we now have. We also lose a sense that we ourselves, and what we have and do, are really good. We expect the rewards from what we do to come in the future rather than from the doing of it, and then become frustrated when most of those dreams cannot be attained. The "future" always continues to lie in the future. Progress is really a euphemism for always believing that what we value and seek today is better than what we valued before or what anyone else has ever sought or valued.

Stewardship, in contrast to progress, elicits attentive care and concern for the present - for understanding its nature and for best developing, nurturing, and protecting its possibilities. Such actions unavoidably insure the best possible future as a byproduct of enjoyment and satisfaction from the present.

The government of a society has a fundamental responsibility – which we have neglected, for stewardship, particularly for the biophysical systems that support our society. It is the only organ of society which can protect those systems and protect future citizens of the society from loss of their needed resources through the profiteering of present citizens. The government's fundamental obligation in this area is to prevent deterioration in the support capacities of the biophysical systems, maintain in stable and sound fashion their ongoing capabilities, and whenever possible extend those capabilities in terms of quality as well as quantity. Recent and past governments, and those who have profited from their actions, must be accountable for loss to present and future citizens and to the biophysical systems themselves from their actions.

AUSTERITY, not affluence.

Austerity is a principle which does not exclude all enjoyments, only those which are distracting from or destructive of personal relatedness. It is part of a more embracing virtue – friendship or joyfulness – and arises from an awareness that things or tools can destroy rather than enhance grace and joyfulness in personal relations. Affluence, in contrast, does not discriminate between what is wise and useful and what is merely possible. Affluence demands impossible endless growth, both because those things necessary for good relations are foregone for unnecessary things, and because many of those unnecessary things act to damage or destroy the good relations that we desire.

PERMANENCE, not profit.

Profit, as a criteria of performance, must be replaced by permanence in a world where irreplaceable resources are in scarce supply. Profit always indicates the immediate use of resources, destroying any ability of a society to sustain itself. The only way to place lighter demands on material resources is to place heavier demands on moral resources. Permanence as a judge of the desirability of actions requires first that those actions contribute to rather than lessen the continuing quality of the society. Permanence in no way excludes fair reward for one's work - but distinguishes the profit a person gains based on loss to others from profit derived from a person's work as contribution to others.

RESPONSIBILITIES, not rights.

A society – or any relationship – based on rights rather than responsibilities is possible only when the actions involved are insignificant enough to not affect others. Our present society is based upon rights rather than responsibilities, and upon competitive distrust and contractual relationships rather than upon the more complex and cooperative kinds of relationships common in other cultures. These relationships have given us the freedom to very quickly extract and use our material wealth, settle a continent, and develop the structure of cities and civilization.

Any enduring relationship, however, must balance rights with responsibilities to prevent destruction of weaker or less aggressive, yet essential, parts of relationships – whether other people, the biosphere that supports our lives, or the various parts of our own personalities.

Distrust or contractual relationships are the easiest to escape and the most expensive to maintain – requiring the development of elaborate and expensive legal and-financial systems – and cannot be the dominant form of relationship in societies that do not have the surplus wealth to afford them. Moral or ethically-based relationships; relationships based on cooperation, trust, and love; and the relationships encompassing more than just work, family, educational, recreational, or spiritual parts of our lives are more rewarding and satisfying to the people involved. They are also more stable in their contribution to society, vastly easier to maintain, and harder to disrupt. They have always been the most common kinds of relationships between people except under the extreme duress of war or growth.

PEOPLE, not professions.
Our wealth has made it possible for us to institutionalize and professionalize many of our individual responsibilities – a process which is inherently ineffective and more costly, which has proven destructive of individual competence and confidence, and which is affordable only when significant surplus of wealth is available.

We have been able to afford going to expensively trained doctors for every small health problem, rather than learning rudiments of medical skills or taking care to prevent health problems. We have been able to afford expensive police protection rather than handling our problems by ourselves or with our neighbors. We have established professional social workers, lawyers, and educators - and required that everyone use their services even for things we could do ourselves and that are wastes of the time and expertise of the professionals. As the wealth that has permitted this becomes less available to us, it will become necessary to deprofessionalize and deinstitutionalize many of these services and again take primary responsibility for them ourselves.

Our institutions have contributed to isolating, buffering, and protecting us from the events of our world. This has on one hand made our lives easier and more secure, and freed us from the continual testing that is part of the dynamic interaction in any natural system. It has also, by these very actions, made us feel isolated, alienated, and rightfully fearful of not being able to meet those continued tests without the aid of our cultural and technical implements.

Our lack of familiarity with the natural processes of our world and uncertainty of our ability to interact with them using our own intuitive wisdom has enslaved us to those implements and degraded us. We can act confidently and with intuitive rightness only when we aren't afraid. We can open ourselves to the living interaction that makes our lives rewarding only when we cease to fear what we can't affect. Fear is only unsureness of our own abilities.

We have to take responsibility ourselves for our own lives, actions, health, and learning. We must also take responsibility ourselves for our community and society. There is no other way to operate any aspect of our lives and society without creating dictatorial power. Such power destroys and prevents the unfolding of human nature and that concentrates the ability to make errors without corrective input. No one else shares our perceptions and perspective on what is occurring and its rightness, wrongness, or alternatives. We are the only ones who can give that perspective to the process of determining and directing the pattern of events.

Our institutions can be tools to serve us only when they arise from and sustain the abilities of individuals and are controlled by them.

BETTER, not bigger.
Quantitative things, because of the ease of their measurement by external means, have been sought and relied upon as measures of success by our institutionally-centered society. We are learning the hard lesson that quantity is no substitute for quality in our lives, that qualitative benefits cannot be externalized, and that a society that wishes better rather than more – and better rather than bigger, must be organized to allow individuals the scope for determining and obtaining what they themselves consider better.

ENOUGH, not more.
We are learning that too much of a good thing is not a good thing. We would often be wiser to determine what is enough rather than how much is possible. When we can learn to be satisfied with the least necessary for happiness, we can lighten our demands on ourselves, on others, and on our surroundings. We can then make new things possible with what we have released from our covetousness. Our consumption ethic has prevented our thinking about enoughness, in part out of fear of unemployment problems arising from reducing our demands.

Employment problems are only a result of arbitrary choices of we have made regarding energy- vs. employment-intensive production processes and regarding the distributing the wealth of our society. Both can be modified with little fundamental difficulty. Our major goal is to be happy with the least effort – with the least production of goods and services necessary, and with the greatest opportunity to employ our time and skills for good rather than for survival. The fewer our wants, the greater our freedom from having to serve them.

LOCALIZATION, not centralization.

Centralization, in all kinds of organization, is important during periods of growth when ability to quickly marshal resources and change and direct an organization is important. It is, however, an expensive and ineffective means for dealing with ongoing operations when an excess of energy to operate the system is unavailable. As effectiveness in resolving problems on the scale and location where they occur becomes more important, organization must move to more localized and less institutionalized ways of operation. Even with sufficient resources, the power concentration of centralized systems overpowers the rights of individuals, and has proved to lead to inevitable deterioration of our quality of life.

The size and centralization of many of our organizations has nothing to do with even alleged economics or benefits of scale, and actually often is associated with diseconomies of scale and deterioration of quality of services. Size breeds size, even where it is counterproductive. It is easiest for any organization to deal with others of the same scale and kind of organization, and to create pressures for other organizations to adapt their own mode of operation.

EQUITIZATION, not urbanization.

Uncontrollable urbanization has accompanied industrialization in every country where it has occurred. The roots of that urbanization, which has occurred in spite of the desires of both the people and the governments involved, has been twofold: the destruction of traditional means of livelihood by energy slaves and the market control of large corporations, and the unequal availability of employment opportunities and educational, medical, and other services. Neither of these conditions are necessary. The inequity of services has resulted from conscious choices to centralize and professionalize services rather than to manage available resources in a way to ensure equal availability of services in rural as well as urban areas. The destruction of traditional patterns of livelihood has been equally based on conscious and unnecessary choices.

Equity is not only possible, but is necessary to restore choices of where and how one lives. It is necessary to restore alternatives to our unaffordably costly urban systems. It can be achieved through introduction of appropriate technology; through control of organization size; by equalizing income and available wealth; by establishing equal access to learning opportunities, health care, justice, and other services; and by assuring everyone the opportunity for meaningful work. It can be achieved by returning to individuals the responsibility and control of their lives, surroundings, and social, economic, and political systems; by ensuring freedom to not consume or depend upon any systems other than one's own abilities; and by encouraging the ownership of the tools of production by the people who do the work, thus increasing the chances of developing a balanced, affluent, and stable society.

WORK, not leisure.

We have considered work to be a negative thing – that the sole function of work was to produce goods and services. To workers it has meant a loss of leisure, something to be minimized while still maintaining income. To the employer it is simply a cost of production, also to be minimized. Yet work is one of our greatest opportunities to contribute to the well-being of ourselves and our community. It is opportunity to utilize and develop our skills and abilities, opportunity to overcome our self-centeredness through joining with other people in common tasks, as well as opportunity to produce the goods and services needed for a dignified existence.

Properly appreciated, work stands in the same relation to the higher faculties as food to the physical body. It nourishes and enlivens us and urges us to produce the best of which we are capable. It furnishes a medium through which to display our scale of values and develop our personality. To strive for leisure rather than work denies that work and leisure are complementary parts of the same living process, and cannot be separated without destroying the joy of work and the bliss of leisure.

From this viewpoint work is something essential to our well being - something that can and ought to be meaningful, the organization of which in ways which are boring, stultifying or nerve-wracking is criminal. Opportunity for meaningful work rather than merely a share of the products of work, needs to be assured to every member of our society.

TOOLS, not MACHINES.

We need to regain the ability to distinguish between technologies which aid and those which destroy our ability to seek the ends we wish. We need to discriminate between what are tools and what are machines. The choice of tools and what they do is at root both philosophical and spiritual. Every technology has its own nature and its own effect upon the world around it. Each arises from, and supports a particular view of our world.

A tool channels work and experiences through our faculties, allowing us to bring to bear upon them the full play of our nature to learn from the work and to infuse it with our purposes and our dreams. Its result is to give the fullest possible opportunity for our physical and mental faculties to experience, experiment and grow. A tool focuses work so that our energy and attention can be fully employed to our chosen purposes.

Our culture has valued devices that are labor saving and require little skill to operate. By those very measures, such devices are machines which rob us of our opportunity to act, experience and grow, and to fill our surroundings with the measure of our growth. We need skill-developing rather than labor-saving technologies.

INDEPENDENCE and INTERDEPENDENCE

Many of the basic values upon which we have tried to build our society have become weakened through the ways they have been interpreted. They face the prospect of further weakening through the pressures inevitable in adapting our society to new conditions.

Independence cannot be maintained when we are dependent upon other people or other nations, we cannot be independent. As long as we are forced to work on other's terms, to consume certain kinds of education to qualify for work, to use automobiles because that kind of transportation system has made even walking dangerous or physically impossible; as long as we are dependent upon fossil fuels to operate our society; as long as we must depend upon resources other than ourselves and the renewable resources of our surroundings.

We have also discovered through the power that our wealth has given us that slavery is as enslaving for the master as for the mastered. With slavery, we all become dependent upon the abilities of the slave, whether the slave is a human, animal, institutional or energy slave. Perhaps most importantly, we forego developing our own capabilities to be self-reliant.

In another sense total independence is never possible, for that means total power, which inevitably collides with the wants and power of others. We are also, in reality, dependent upon the natural systems that convert the sun's energy into the food upon which we live. Totally independent individuals may have freedom from organization, but have no special value, no special mission, no special contribution and no necessary role in the energy flows and relationships of a society. Such freedom results in little respect or value for the individual. Our success and survival on this planet also must recognize the total interdependence that exists between us and the health, disease, wealth, happiness, anger, and frustrations of the others with whom we share this planet.

Two things are important. We must have the capability for self-sufficiency – in order to have options, alternatives, self-confidence, and knowledge of how things are related and work and to be able to lighten our demands on others. We must also have the ability to contribute our special skills to the development of interdependent relationships which can benefit all. Trade – as giving of surplus, of what is not necessary - is the only viable resolution of the interrelated problems of independence, interdependence, and slavery.

As we begin to actually make changes, the things we come to find of value are almost the opposite of what we value today. What contributes to stability and soundness and to valued relationships is exactly what prevents and hinders disruption, change, and growth. Until recently, change and growth have both been necessary and desired under the conditions we have experienced. Now, however, meaningful work, localized economies, diversity and richness of employment and community, and controllable, clever, human centered technologies become important. Common sense and intuition will be recognized again as more valuable than armies of computers.

Community will become more important than individualism and our present actions seen as insupportably selfish. Strong roots and relationships will become more important than mobility. Buildings and equipment with long life and lower total costs rather than low initial costs will be favored. Cooperation will be seen as more positive, wiser, and less costly than competition. Skill-using will replace labor-saving. We will soon discover that all our present sciences and principles are not unbiased, but are built upon values promoting growth rather than stability, and will need to be modified when quantitative growth is no longer possible.

---

[1] From SHARING SMALLER PIES, Tom Bender, 1974.

Appendix C
Vitality and Affordability of Higher Education[1]

The basic structure of our higher education system has been unchanged since before the printing press was invented, when teachers were the sole source of learning content. An estimated two-thirds of undergraduate credit hours uses a classroom lecture-style structure. In it an instructor covers virtually the same material as in the texts used. The same coverage is repeated by other instructors in other sections, other years, and other institutions. This redundancy is amazingly wasteful of both faculty and financial resources, as well as student time.

There are at least four major goals of our higher education systems:

* Access to learning resources
* Accrediting learning achievement
* Job competency certification
* Research

These are today interwoven in an instructor-centered, course-based system, in which faculty workloads and salaries underwrite major free time for personal research; individual faculty do testing of student achievement; course requirements are prescribed for degrees giving access to specific fields of work; a lecture-centered system provides very expensive redundancy of learning resources; and faculty are hired based on expertise in their field of work, not competency in teaching, testing, research, or certification.

Where publicly funded, there is rarely discussion of priorities for the research that is supported. In private colleges, students' tuition actually pays as much for faculty to do their own research as to teach!

Advanced students perform unpaid or underpaid teaching, testing, and research which appears to be done by faculty. Unnecessary coursework is imposed on students with differing prior experience and needs. And increasingly, students find they have to undertake additional study and undergo an additional testing to be allowed to work in many fields.

Looking at those major goals and asking what more direct paths might exist to achieve them, we find that significant alternatives and opportunities for change are exploding around us. Video, audio, computer and CD-ROM training programs, as well as written materials are available in an expanding range of subject areas. Some of these are highly refined, with verified effectiveness of the learning processes being used. More than 100 colleges now offer at least partial non-residency degree work, and credit for non-academic experience. Students are increasingly finding more effective learning alternatives to a college education – because of both cost and relevance. Public and private funding sources are questioning the return on investment in higher education.

The following outlines a procedure for gradual or rapid modification which would allow our system to:

* Become user- rather than supplier-oriented

* Be individually tailored to each person's needs

* Evolve into a resource for life-long learning

* Develop global resource-access capabilities

* Use all individuals' capabilities more fully

* Achieve an order of magnitude improvement in financial effectiveness

I. ACCESS TO LEARNING RESOURCES

☐ Replace the "live" lecture format of 50% of undergraduate college courses with a high quality videotape (or equivalent) medium[1]

* With the average American now having spent more hours in front of a TV before entering kindergarten than is needed to earn a college degree, the medium cannot be ignored as a

potential learning environment. Videotapes of college lectures can provide a roughly comparable experience at a small fraction of the cost, and with greater ease of access. Development of higher-quality videos, such as the PBS Planet Earth series, can frequently provide a better learning experience than the standard lecture format.

Beginning video development with introductory courses in each field and moving into more advanced areas would allow greatest numerical impact early in the program. Initial "talking head" taping of present lectures can be upgraded, after the first year, self-funded through using released staff time. Or staff funding can be used to develop improved, higher quality videos.

Assuming each lecture course each university is offered only once yearly, even a "talking head" videotape program could represent up to a 90% elimination of resource waste over a ten year period. Multiplying that by the number of universities in the world gives a rough projection of the potential resources that could be released to more effective use.

☐ Develop an open-access satellite/cable/internet/ TV/VCR/CD-ROM distribution system for instant global availability.

* This distribution system multiplies access exponentially at extremely low cost. With VCR's, Internet, or CD-ROM, access need not be synchronized with time zones and viewing times.

* With satellite/internet access, program libraries may be developed at any remote location, or programs adapted and modified to local needs and conditions.

☐ Develop the materials in separate visual / caption / verbal "overlays" to permit optimum adaptation in other languages.

* The low cost of reformatting would give significantly lower costs for multiple-language use.

☐ Develop a multi-track international process for developing videos in order to stimulate quality competition.

* In-house planning and production of tapes (particularly at beginning to set quality standards).

* Purchase of programs, tapes, etc. for as-is or modified use.

    * Competitions for new programs, proposals, etc.

    * Awards for most successful programs.

    * Both peer-group and independent processes for planning and review of programs.

    * Contract production and/or planning under in-house review.

☐ Develop a family of "gate-keepers" and other techniques to facilitate effective access to the desired resources.

    * Too many resources can be intimidating and consume too much time and effort in selecting an appropriate resource. Experience has shown the importance of respected reference sources for "best book or tape in the field," for what areas should be studied to prepare for specific interests, and for giving a taste of what reviewed resources have to offer. The Whole Earth Catalog, Literary Reviews, certain mail book catalogs, and newsletters in various fields have demonstrated the value of such "gatekeepers" and how to perform that function well. These should track books and other resources as well as "college-lecture-equivalent" videos.

    * Video programs should include tables of contents / indexes at the beginning of the tapes, on boxes, and available separately to simplify access and review of specific segments.

    The next two proposals separate the learning process from the process of demonstrating competency in subject areas, and provide lower cost systematized evaluation.

II. ACCREDITING LEARNING ACHIEVEMENT

☐ Separate the process of testing knowledge and accomplishment in academic fields from completing resident college courses.

    * Knowledge and accomplishment increasingly comes from a sources outside traditional college classrooms. Separating accrediting of learning achieved from the taking of residency courses has been the successful basis of many European higher education systems for years. Over one hundred

schools in the U.S. – running the gamut of credibility – now offer degrees by home study. The New York State *Regents Credit Bank* provides credible evaluation of academic records and equivalency examinations available to people anywhere in the world.

* CLEP (College-Level Examination Program)[2], and PEP (Proficiency Examination Program)[3] together currently administer standardized equivalency examinations in more than seventy-five course areas, at a cost of from $30-$125 per course. These programs could be expanded or supplemented to cover other areas or evaluation techniques.

* Both self-testing and outside-testing needs to be included. Self-testing to ensure effectiveness and thoroughness of learning, and outside-testing for validation to others. A clear program of equivalency testing and accreditation encourages students to find diverse and cost-effective ways to learn and puts the emphasis properly on the learning achieved itself.

III. JOB COMPETENCY CERTIFICATION

☐ Develop or expand, where needed, certification programs for new workers in various fields, combining accredited or self-studied academic courses, work experience, apprentice training, oral examinations as pertinent.

* Few would claim that *either* resident academic training or equivalency exams ensure the necessary training for many fields of work. Certification separate from academic training is required in a wide variety of fields. Improved certification requirements combined with supervised apprentice programs can offer a meshing of academic study, work training, and income for students preparing for work in various fields.

IV. RESEARCH

The present academic structure provides partial funding for university staff to do personal research. Such research is often vital, and should not be eliminated by the inevitable development of lower cost delivery of learning resources.

☐ Develop a prioritization and funding process for public supported research.

> * Priorities and funding should be developed separately by governmental jurisdictions, by universities, by academic discipline, by problems, and by geographic area.

☐ Develop a dated on-line index to:

> * **Research in progress** Prevent unnecessary duplication. Encourage "networking" of people working in related areas. Provide medium for interconnecting projects. Provide opportunity for public dialog on most effective avenues of research.

> * **"Research needed" proposals** Person suggesting research and its potential benefit would establish priority for the idea and get equal credit for its results. List could be used to develop funding. Others could propose alternate research to achieve the same ends.

☐ Develop a "sabbatical funding" process for 'support' of non-funded research.

> * This should not be limited to academic personnel.

V. REFOCUSING EXISTING ACADEMIC CAMPUSES AND COMMUNITIES

> * Focus on residency-needed courses requiring hands-on studio work, interactive study, tutorials, labs, language, co-learner groups, field trips, research frontiers and graduate programs. A "Community of Learners" should be sought rather than a faculty/student structure.

> * Develop student-based access, study groups, tutorial aid, etc. to supplement print and electronic resources.

> * Attract the best foreign students, and create a strong focus on international and intercultural training for global employment opportunities and education needs.

VI. REVIEWING RESOURCE ALLOCATION

Making more effective learning resources available releases financial resources for reallocation. That decision is a public and political one, but the boundaries within which reallocation can occur include:

* Funding reduction

* Fee reductions and wider access to more students

* Increased faculty research time

* More individualized teaching, course research, etc.

* New courses and programs

The development of alternative learning resources and access routes is burgeoning today, and unless addressed directly, will force changes in higher education without the opportunity to properly address the full range of issues involved.[4] For-profit learning modules are unlikely to provide the depth of academic freedom, currency of information, and open dialog of a system that incorporates all participants in its design and operation.

Together these proposals establish the framework for a more flexible, dynamic and cost-effective higher education system which acknowledges and builds upon the proven successes of our present system. This framework allows the expanding variety of learning processes available to us today to take their proper place beside the traditional process of classroom lecture It recognizes the opportunities and challenges of our new global society, and helps higher education systems carve out a viable role in that society. Perhaps most importantly, it demonstrates that learning is something that can be shared with everyone, with benefits to all.

Access to learning resources is a primary goal of higher education. The cost of achieving that can be reduced *more* than an order-of-magnitude, while at the same time reducing administrative and facility costs, and making far better use of human resources. Separating out accrediting learning achievement, job competency certification, and research allows those issues to be addressed directly and in a more comprehensive mode also. Almost as a bonus, we can make that same access to learning resources available on a global basis, in an open structure, and under the control of the people who want it.

Education is an important basis of success in the coming century. Its vitality, effectiveness, affordability and appropriateness need to be ensured and expanded if we are to be among the successful. What we truly need and seek, however, is not education, or facts, or information, or knowledge – but *wisdom*. That we have to forge individually – no education system can provide us that. A system based on individual initiative and needs can, nonetheless, encourage us to develop our own wisdom.

A growing number of technologies are developing which may offer potential application in specific subject or process areas. Some are proven, some quite untested. For simplicity's sake, we focus here on only one - videotapes. This is a familiar, proven, and understandable technology, so we can more clearly focus on the elements necessary to generate an effective system. We could equally well include books, fax, computers or tele-conferencing as parts of the technological medium, but the simple video element will demonstrate some particularly valuable attributes. In practice, other technologies can be added and incorporated as their benefit is proven.

---

[1] *"Vitality and Affordability of Higher Education,"* Tom Bender, Oct. 1993. Prepared as part of the State of Oregon's Review of Higher Education.
[2] Offered by the College Entrance Examination Board.
[3] Offered by the American College Testing Program.
[4] See, for example, "Digital Diplomas" by Eyal Press and Jennifer Washburn, MOTHER JONES, Jan/Feb. 2001.

FURTHER READING

von Weizsacher, Lovins and Lovins – FACTOR FOUR, and Lovins, Lovins & Hawken –NATURAL CAPITALISM. These two books document over a hundred examples of order-of-magnitude resource productivity gains in executed projects.

Schumacher, E.F. – SMALL IS BEAUTIFUL, and A GUIDE FOR THE PER PLEXED. Schumacher's "Buddhist Economics" in SMALL IS BEAU-TIFUL is must reading for understanding the pivotal role of values and the sacred in determining the nature of our economics.

Somé, Malidoma – OF WATER AND THE SPIRIT, and THE HEALING WIS-DOM OF AFRICA. The role of the sacred, community, and ritual in modern African culture – vital perspectives on our own.

Armstrong, Karen – ISLAM: A SHORT HISTORY. Compassionate scholarship on a spiritual-centered culture. Chapter on religious fundamental-ism in the modern world is a must read for today's world.

Bender, Tom – SILENCE, SONG & SHADOWS, and BUILDING WITH THE BREATH OF LIFE. Impact of the sacred and life-force energy in de-sign and construction of our surroundings today.

BIBLIOGRAPHY

A

Alternatives to Growth Oregon, <www.AGOregon.org>.
Armstrong, Karen – ISLAM: A Short History, Modern Library, 2000.

B

Ballard, Charles and Medema, Steven – *"The Marginal Efficiency Effect of Taxes and Subsidies . . ."*, Michigan State University, 1992.
Bender, Tom – *"Amazon Student Family Housing,"* April, 1994.
——, *"Automate the Rich, Not the Poor,"* RAIN Magazine, 1980.
——, *"Bank of Astoria: Building Community Sustainability,"* 2001.
——, *"Borrowing Trouble,"* 1993.
——, *"Building Real Wealth,"* May. 1993. Reprinted in IN CONTEXT, Issue 44, July, 1996.
——, *BUILDING VALUE*, Office of California State Architect, 1976.
——, BUILDING WITH THE BREATH OF LIFE, Fire River Press, 2000.
——, *"Cosmic Economics,"* with Joel Schatz, OERP, 1974.
——, *"Eco-building II,"* ENVIRONMENTAL BUILDING NEWS, July 1996; IN CONTEXT, July 1996.
——, *"Economics Where People DO Matter,"* RAIN Magazine, April 1979.
——, *"Emerging Energy Policy Principles,"* with OERP, 1974.
——, *"Endgame Analysis,"* Nov. 1990, IN CONTEXT, July 1996.
——, THE HEART OF PLACE, Fire River Press, 1993.

———, *"The End of Nuclear War,"* 1986.

———, *"Hidden Costs of Housing,"* RAIN Magazine, Mar/Apr 1984. Reprinted in UTNE READER, Summer 1984; SUN TIMES, Nov/Dec 1984; ALTERNATIVE PRESS ANNUAL, 1984.

———, *"Improving the Economic Value of Coastal Public Forest Lands,"* Dec. 1994, IN CONTEXT, July 1996.

———, *"Independence?,"* with OERP, 1974.

———, *"It's Oil Right, Folks! There's Good Times Ahead,"* SOLAR ENERGY ASSOCIATION OF OREGON, 1996.

———, *"Izu Principles,"* Oct. 1994.

———, *"Jobs, Humbug!"* RAIN Magazine, April 1978.

———, *"Let Fantasies Be Fantasies,"* RAIN Magazine, April 1977.

———, *LIVING LIGHTLY: Energy Conservation in Housing,* October 1973.

———, *"Northern Lights,"* WINTER CITIES FORUM, 1986.

———, *"Rent-Alls,"* AORTA Bulletin, Jan 1995. Reprinted in IN CONTEXT, Issue 44, July 1996.

———, *"Sacred Roots of Sustainable Design,"* Sept. 1995.

———, *"Seek Wisdom, Not Vengeance,"* DAILY ASTORIAN, Sept. 21, 2001.

———, *"Sewage is Art - The Healing of Place with Chi,"* June 1995.

———, *SHARING SMALLER PIES,* 1975; reprinted in RAIN Magazine, April '75 and Oct. '83; New Age Journal, Nov. '75; THE FUTURIST, 1976; RESETTLING AMERICA, Gary Coates, ed., 1981; UTNE READER, Fall, 1987.

———, *"Shedding A Skin That No Longer Fits,"* Mar. 1996. Reprinted in IN CONTEXT, July 1996.

———, SILENCE, SONG & SHADOWS, Fire River Press, 2000.

———, *"Simple Prices,"* Feb. 1996.

———, *"Some Questions We Haven't Asked,"* 1994.

———, *"Suburban Renewal,"* RAIN Magazine, April 1978.

———, *"Survival in the Suburbs,"* SURVIVAL TOMORROW, 1981.

———, *"Technology is Not the Problem and Not the Answer"*, RAIN Magazine, May, 1977.

———, *"Ten Easy Pieces of a Better World,"* DAILY ASTORIAN, Oct. 31, 2001.

———, *"The Third Pig is Always Fattest,"* RAIN Magazine, May, 1977.

, *"True Security,"* RAIN Magazine, Oct. 1982

———, *"Unexpected Gifts,"* 1996.

———, *"Vitality and Affordability of Higher Education,"* Oct. 1993. Republished in IN CONTEXT, July 1996.

———, *"Work and Leisure,"* MANAS, April 1983.

Benyas, Janine – BIOMIMICRY, Wm. Morrow & Co., 1997.

Burckhardt, Titus – CHARTRES AND THE BIRTH OF THE CATHEDRAL, 1962.

C

California, State of – *"Investing for Prosperity."*

D

Daly, Herman E., and Cobb, John – FOR THE COMMON GOOD, Beacon Press, 1989.

———, STEADY-STATE ECONOMICS, W.H. Freeman, 1977.

———, ed. – TOWARD A STEADY-STATE ECONOMY, W.H. Freeman, 1973.

———, and Townsend, Kenneth N., ed. – VALUING THE EARTH: Economics, Ecology, Ethics, and M.I.T. Press, 1993.

DuBoulay, Shirley – TUTU: ARCHBISHOP WITHOUT FRONTIERS, Hodder & Stoughton, 1996.

E

Elizabeth, Lynne and Adams, Cassandra, ed. – ALTERNATIVE CONSTRUCTION, John Wiley & Sons, 2000.

F

Freidel, David, Schele, Linda, and Parker, Joy – MAYA COSMOS, Wm. Morrow & Co, 1993.

Fodor, Eben – BETTER, NOT BIGGER, New Society, 1999.

H

Harvey, Hal and Shuman, Mike – SECURITY WITHOUT WAR, Westview, 1993.

Hawken, Paul, Lovins, Amory and L. Hunter – NATURAL CAPITALISM, Little, Brown & Company, 1999.

Henderson, Hazel – PARADIGMS IN PROGRESS: Life Beyond Economics, Knowledge Systems, 1991.

——, BUILDING A WIN-WIN WORLD: Life Beyond Global Economic Warfare, Berrett-Koehler, 1996.

J

Jensen, Derrick – *"Neighborhood Bully: Ramsey Clark On American Militarism,"* THE SUN, August, 2001.

Johnson, George – *"Scientists Push Quantum Theory Closer to Reality,"* NYT News Service, Oct.17, 2001.

K

Kwitney, Jonathan – ENDLESS ENEMIES: The Making of an Unfriendly World, Penguin, 1986.

Kummarappa, J.C. – ECONOMICS OF PERMANENCE, Sarva-Seva Sangh Publications, 1958.

L

THE LAST STRAW, Issue #33, Spring 2001.

Lovins and Hawken, *"Beyond Natural Capitalism,"* <www.natcap.org>.

Lovins, Amory and L. Hunter – BRITTLE POWER: Energy Strategy for National Security, Brick House, 1982.

——, and Hawken, Paul – NATURAL CAPITALISM, Little, Brown & Company, 1999.

Lovins, Amory – *"Tunneling through the Cost Barrier,"* RMI Newsletter, Summer 1997.

M

McKibben, Bill – HOPE, HUMAN AND WILD, Little, Brown, 1995.

N

——, *"The Experimental Verification of Quantum Teleportation,"* NATURE, Dec. 1997.

NW Environmental Technology Laboratories, Inc., with Mathematical Sciences, Inc., and Energy, Inc. – ENERGY 1990 STUDY, Initial Report (7 volumes), prepared for the City of Seattle Department of Lighting (now Seattle City Light), 1976.

O

Odum, H.T. – ECOLOGICAL AND GENERAL SYSTEMS, Univ. Press of Colorado, 1994.

———, and Odum, E.C. – ENERGY BASIS FOR MAN AND NATURE, McGraw Hill, 1976.

———, ENVIRONMENT, POWER, AND SOCIETY, Wiley-Interscience, 1970.

P

Press, Eyal and Washburn, Jennifer – *"Digital Diplomas,"* MOTHER JONES, Jan/Feb. 2001.

———, *"Ouroboros Project,"* POPULAR SCIENCE, Dec. 1975.

Q

Querido, René – THE GOLDEN AGE OF CHARTRES, Floris Books, 1987.

R

REDEFINING PROGRESS – *"Tax Waste, Not Work,"* 1992.

Repetto, Bob and Dower, Roger – *"Green Fees,"* WORLD RESOURCES INSTITUTE, 1992.

RMI SOLUTIONS NEWSLETTER, Spring 2001.

S

Sant, Roger L. – LEAST-COST ENERGY PLANNING, 1974.

Schatz, Joel and Bender, Tom – *"Cosmic Economics,"* Office of Energy Research and Planning (OERP), Governor's Office, State of Oregon, 1974.

———, *"Emerging Energy Policy Principles,"* OERP, 1974.

———, *"Independence?"* OERP, 1974.

Schumacher, E.F., A GUIDE FOR THE PERPLEXED, Harper and Row, 1977.

———, *"Buddhist Economics,"* in ASIA: A Handbook, ed. Guy Wint, Anthony Blond Ltd, 1966. Reprinted in ENVIRONMENTAL DESIGN PRIMER, Tom Bender, 1973 and SMALL IS BEAUTIFUL, E.F. Schumacher, 1974, 1999.

———, SMALL IS BEAUTIFUL, Harper Collins, 1974; Hartley & Marks, 1999.

Shilling, A. Gary – DEFLATION, McGraw-Hill, 1999.

Steen, Athena and Bill – THE BEAUTY OF STRAW BALE HOMES, Chelsea Green, 2001.

Somé, Malidoma – OF WATER AND THE SPIRIT, Tarcher/Putnam, 1994.

———, THE HEALING WISDOM OF AFRICA, Tarcher/Putnam, 1998.

———, RITUAL, Swan/Raven & Co, 1993.

V

von Weizsächer, Ernst, and Lovins, Amory and L. Hunter – FACTOR FOUR, Earthscan, 1997.

W

Weisman, Alan – GAVIOTAS, Chelsea Green, 1998.

Wigg, Mark – *"The Economics of Sustainable Forestry,"* SOCIETY OF AMERICAN FORESTERS, 1989.

Index

FIRE RIVER PRESS
Quick Order Form

Telephone Inquiries: (503) 368-6294
Email Inquiries: fireriverpress@nehalemtel.net
Postal Orders: *FIRE RIVER PRESS,* PO Box 397, Manzanita OR 97130
Please send payment with orders.

PLEASE SEND THE FOLLOWING BOOKS:

( ) copies of *Silence, Song & Shadows* @ $27
( ) copies of *Building with the Breath of Life* @ $28
( ) copies of *Learning to Count What REALLY Counts* @ $22

SHIPPING: US – Currently $5 for the first book, $3 for each additional book.
INTERNATIONAL – Inquire for current rates.

NAME: _____

ADDRESS: _____

CITY: _____ STATE: _____ ZIP: _____

COUNTRY: _____

TELEPHONE: _____ E-MAIL ADDRESS: _____

FIRE RIVER PRESS
Quick Order Form

Telephone Inquiries: (503) 368-6294
Email Inquiries: fireriverpress@nehalemtel.net
Postal Orders: *FIRE RIVER PRESS,* PO Box 397, Manzanita OR 97130
Please send payment with orders.

PLEASE SEND THE FOLLOWING BOOKS:

( ) copies of *Silence, Song & Shadows* @ $27
( ) copies of *Building with the Breath of Life* @ $28
( ) copies of *Learning to Count What REALLY Counts* @ $22

SHIPPING: US – Currently $5 for the first book, $3 for each additional book.
INTERNATIONAL – Inquire for current rates.

NAME: _____

ADDRESS: _____

CITY: _____ STATE: _____ ZIP: _____

COUNTRY: _____

TELEPHONE: _____ E-MAIL ADDRESS: _____